"Considering pertinent issues associated with qualitative criminological research in contemporary settings, Rahman and Deuchar draw upon their own experience of working with hard-to-reach and marginalised populations to raise difficult, yet must have conversations, concerning an ever-evolving field of ethics. In doing so, the authors offer both practical recommendations and direction for the future of ethics. The work is most certainly a must read for anyone seeking to undertake cutting edge criminological research."

Dr Robert McLean, *University of the West of Scotland*

"*Ethics in Qualitative Criminological Research: Risks, Boundaries, Emotions, and Reflexivity* offers unique and invaluable insights into navigating the ethical complexities of qualitative research in criminology – of which there are many. Drawing from rich literature and personal experiences, Rahman and Deuchar provide practical solutions to ethical dilemmas, making it an essential guide for students, researchers, and practitioners alike."

Associate Professor Amin Asfari, *Regis University*

"Research ethics are probably the most important but most neglected topic in methods training. As such it is fantastic to see research ethics front and centre in this engaging new text by two experienced researchers."

Professor Shadd Maruna, *University of Liverpool*

"*Ethics in Qualitative Criminological Research: Risks, Boundaries, Emotions, and Reflexivity* is an insightful work of many qualities. Rahman and Deuchar have 'walked the walk' before writing such as book and the end product is a rounded and admirably clear account of the often unclear boundaries in the complex landscape of criminological research. This is an essential read especially for early career criminologists and other social scientists, who will also find wise, practical, and ethical solutions."

Professor Georgios A. Antonopoulos, *Northumbria University*

Ethics in Qualitative Criminological Research

Providing academic insights, reflections, and practical guidance on ethically conducting qualitative criminological research, this book emphasizes real-life examples to navigate research risks, boundaries, and emotions, while spotlighting reflexivity as a pivotal tool for qualitative inquiries, serving as an ethical compass throughout the research process.

By engaging with this book, readers will be exposed to critical themes of managing risks, including physical harm and psychological trauma, navigating boundaries, dealing with the intense emotions that surface during research, and the importance of reflexivity in qualitative criminological research. The themes are illustrated through real-life examples that the authors have encountered during their fieldwork, using reflexive practices to highlight how they were able to ethically deal with unforeseen challenges. By presenting solutions, asking critical questions, and offering practical recommendations, the book guides readers on mitigating ethical issues, and provides a comprehensive approach to conducting research responsibly and ethically.

Ethics in Qualitative Criminological Research will be useful for undergraduate and postgraduate students, academic researchers and practitioners with an interest in conducting research, and pracademics occupying both practitioner and academic roles.

Mohammed Rahman is Senior Lecturer in the College of Law, Social and Criminal Justice at Birmingham City University, UK. He is also Network Expert for the Global Initiative Against Transnational Organized Crime.

Ross Deuchar is Professor of Criminology and Criminal Justice in the School of Education and Social Sciences at the University of the West of Scotland, UK.

Ethics in Qualitative Criminological Research

Risks, Boundaries, Emotions, and Reflexivity

Mohammed Rahman and Ross Deuchar

Routledge
Taylor & Francis Group
LONDON AND NEW YORK

First published 2025
by Routledge
4 Park Square, Milton Park, Abingdon, Oxon OX14 4RN

and by Routledge
605 Third Avenue, New York, NY 10158

Routledge is an imprint of the Taylor & Francis Group, an informa business

© 2025 Mohammed Rahman and Ross Deuchar

The right of Mohammed Rahman and Ross Deuchar to be identified as authors of this work has been asserted in accordance with sections 77 and 78 of the Copyright, Designs and Patents Act 1988.

British Library Cataloguing-in-Publication Data
A catalogue record for this book is available from the British Library

ISBN: 978-1-032-29929-7 (hbk)
ISBN: 978-1-032-30368-0 (pbk)
ISBN: 978-1-003-30474-6 (ebk)

DOI: 10.4324/9781003304746

Typeset in Times New Roman
by Deanta Global Publishing Services, Chennai, India

Contents

Foreword

James A. Densley

Too often, methods books are penned by academics whose feet, metaphorically speaking, rarely touch the ground of the complex and unpredictable landscapes they study. These texts, while academically rigorous, float above the practical complexities and ethical quandaries faced by researchers embedded in the raw fabric of their environments. *Ethics in Criminological Research: Risks, Boundaries, Emotions, and Reflexivity* stands apart because it is authored by researchers who are not just observers from an ivory tower, but who are deeply entrenched in the very essence of fieldwork. In this book, Mohammed Rahman and Ross Deuchar draw upon their extensive frontline experience in criminological research, including studies I had the honor of collaborating on (e.g., Deuchar & Densley, 2023; Rahman, et al., 2022), affording readers the benefit of a deeply engaged and empathetic approach to scholarship that I have personally witnessed.

This book is more than just a collection of methodologies; it is a testament to the belief that at the core of criminological research is the unwavering principle of ethics. The authors bring to the forefront the critical themes of managing risks, including physical harm and psychological trauma, navigating boundaries, dealing with the intense emotions that surface during research, and the importance of reflexivity in our work. Through the prism of their vast experiences with homeless populations, incarcerated persons, delinquent youth, people embedded in street gangs and organized criminal networks, and individuals grappling with drug addiction and mental ill health, Rahman and Deuchar illuminate the multifaceted humanity of those often relegated to the shadows of society with unparalleled authenticity.

In the heart of criminological research lies a profound commitment to understanding the intricate web of human experiences—those of the marginalized, the misunderstood, and often, the misrepresented. This book is a beacon of light in the dense fog that often surrounds the moral complexities that students and scholars doing this work commonly face. It underscores the practical utility of ethics in research, not as an abstract concept, but as a living, breathing principle that guides every decision we make. After all, ethical standards are not static; they evolve in response to societal changes, legal developments, and technological innovations. The modern age demands that researchers remain agile, continuously updating their ethical frameworks to reflect new challenges and ensure their work contributes positively to an ever-changing world; because ethical lapses, not only in conduct but in the presentation and use of research findings, will only erode public trust in the science needed to make informed policy decisions that benefit society.

As the authors note, ethics in research is about giving voice to people's stories with the utmost respect and sensitivity, ensuring that we do not pathologize the individuals we study, but rather seek to understand their experiences in all their complexity. It is about capturing the essence of their lives accurately, providing a platform for their narratives to be shared with the world. The case examples in this book, drawn from the authors' prior research, are not merely narratives; they are windows into the lives of individuals who, despite being labeled as "offenders" and "victims," are fundamentally human beings with stories that demand to be understood without prejudice. This book brilliantly captures the essence of conducting research with a heart, emphasizing the importance of not just listening to people's stories, but truly hearing them.

The journey of criminological research is fraught with challenges—legal, logistical, and even liminal (i.e., the thresholds where traditional rules and norms may not apply, and where roles and identities can be fluid)—not least of which is the trauma researchers encounter and experience as they delve into the lives of those they study. My own research into the life histories of mass shooters across the United States (Peterson & Densley, 2021) has unfolded as a voyage through the tumultuous seas of human emotions—encompassing anger, grief, guilt, and the relentless pursuit of understanding "why?" Spending time in communities irrevocably transformed by tragedy and with the families of incarcerated perpetrators and deceased victims, shooting survivors, and first responders, I have experienced firsthand the weight of the sorrow and the resilience of the human spirit. *Ethics in Criminological Research* courageously addresses these challenges, offering strategies for researchers to care for their positionality and emotional well-being while conducting research that is responsible and recognizes the dignity of every individual we encounter.

Standing on the threshold of a new era in criminological research, marked by rapid technological advancements like generative Artificial Intelligence, and changing societal norms, where researchers can inadvertently exert influence through social media or other platforms, affecting public discourse and the lives of research participants, the ethical guidelines laid out in this book are more important than ever. To the future generations of researchers who will navigate these uncharted waters, let this book be your North Star. May you conduct your research with courage, compassion, and an unwavering commitment to ethics, for in the end, it is not just about understanding human behavior but about contributing to a more just and empathetic world.

James A. Densley
Professor and Department Chair of Criminology and Criminal Justice
Metropolitan State University
Saint Paul, Minnesota
USA

References

Deuchar, R., & Densley, J. (2023). Exploring the intersection of drug addiction and mental ill-health in Scottish prisons: a qualitative study of incarcerated men. *Journal of Drug Issues.* doi: 10.1177/00220426231161282.

Peterson, J., & Densley, J. (2021). *The violence project: how to stop a mass shooting epidemic.* Abrams Press.

Rahman, M., McLean, R., Deuchar, R., & Densley, J. (2022). Who are the enforcers? The motives and methods of muscle for hire in West Scotland and the West Midlands. Trends in Organized Crime, 25(1), 108–129. doi: 10.1007/s12117-020-09382-y.

Acknowledgements

Al-hamdulilāh.

Like much of my academic work, this book would not have been possible without the contributions of those who allowed me to delve into their lives. While I cannot name them individually due to confidentiality, their invaluable input is deeply appreciated.

Special thanks to the Routledge team, particularly Lydia de Cruz and Medha Malaviya, for recognising the significance of this work and for supporting me during recent academic hurdles.

I extend my sincere appreciation to Dr Martin Glynn, who served as a critical sounding board for the duration of the book. Thank you, Professor James Densley, for writing the foreword, and to Dr Robert McLean, Professors Amin Asfari, Georgios Antonopoulos, and Shadd Maruna, for your endorsements.

Lastly, a heartfelt thanks to my parents for instilling in me strong ethics, to my wife for her unwavering steadfastness and encouragement, especially during tough times, and to our newborn, whose future we envision in a more ethical and civilised world.

Mohammed Rahman

I would like to thank all of the research participants I have worked with over the years who gave up their time to share some of the most personal and often traumatic experiences with me – it is a real privilege to be able to spend time with some of the most marginalised in society and without their willingness to open up emotionally to me, this work would not have been possible.

My sincere gratitude goes to the esteemed academics who have endorsed this work for us – Professor James Densley, Dr Robert McLean, Professors Amin Asfari, Georgios Antonopoulos, and Shadd Maruna.

To my wife Karen and son Alan – as always, without their endless love and support I would not have been able to complete this work.

Finally, I would like to dedicate my contribution to this book to the late Douglas Weir, formally Professor and at one time Dean of the Faculty of Education, University of Strathclyde. As my PhD supervisor and academic mentor, he always provided me with unwavering encouragement and support and first instilled my passion for research and academic publishing. Without his guidance and support in my early academic career, professionally I would not be where I am today.

Ross Deuchar

1 Philosophy, Ethics, Research Governance, and Reflexivity

Introduction

Philosophy and Ethics

The word 'philosophy' for most people may come across as quite intimidating. Many may view it as a lofty discipline that is beyond their reach of understanding. Generally, in daily life, philosophy is more of an *active* pursuit than a *body of knowledge* that is largely discussed within intellectual settings. Our decision-making in daily life is contingent upon our beliefs and opinions. This means that we *do* philosophy in our quest for knowledge and wisdom. Fundamentally, it is the etymology of the word *philosophia*, which in Ancient Greek means a lover of wisdom (Deigh, 2010). Great thinkers who have formally challenged the intellectual curiosity and thinking of people through a body of knowledge often explore life's big questions to better understand what we should do at a fundamental level and beyond.

Given the sheer size of philosophy, it would be impossible to cover all aspects here. Also, given the primary audience for this book, it would be an unfeasible task. The volume of philosophy at our disposal is vast. Some of the established forms of philosophy are Eastern, ancient, medieval, renaissance, modern, political, twentieth century, and postmodern (Poulton, 2021). In the present day, philosophy continues to evolve, largely because of global technological advancements, as well as ongoing contributions by global intellects. The evolution of artificial intelligence, for instance, presents a challenge around notions of consciousness, and therefore becomes a pressing area of philosophical inquiry. Chalmers (1996) theorises that consciousness has a universal quality that can be found in everything to a certain degree. This then raises important questions about the ethical implications of artificial intelligence, which is entrenched deeply in daily human life (see Chapter 5 for further insight). Crenshaw's (1989) pioneering work on intersectionality drew upon how legislation reacts to issues that consist of gender and racial discrimination. While some have challenged the methodological aspects of intersectional scholarship (Carbin & Edenheim, 2013; Bilge, 2013), others have praised how intersectional philosophy has helped evolve activist movements,

DOI: 10.4324/9781003304746-1

specifically in relation to feminism and racial inequalities (Jibrin & Salem, 2015). Philosophers are dynamic thinkers, and this has been the case since the origins of the discipline.

Socrates (c. 470–399 BCE), who is widely referred to as one of the seminal thinkers of Western philosophy, was particularly interested in the ethical considerations of human life, rather than the material world that occupied the work of his predecessors. He was not a formal scholar. Rather what we know about his work is only through the account of others, namely his student, Plato (c. 428–348 BCE) (Poulton, 2021). Socrates believed in establishing the truth for anything in life, and the primary method to achieve this is to keep asking questions. For him, virtue is knowledge, and to live a virtuous life is to live a good life.

Through the work of Socrates, we can establish parallels with a branch of philosophy known as ethics. Also known as moral philosophy, ethics deals with the moral principles of daily life. It is a strand of philosophy that consolidates, upholds, and tackles right and wrong conduct. Through ethics, we can attempt to define conceptual understandings of good and evil – right and wrong – crime and justice – virtue and vice. The etymology of the word ethics derives from the Greek word *ethikos*, which is to show moral character (Poulton, 2021). Modern philosophy largely categorises ethics into three types: meta-ethics, applied ethics, and normative ethics. Meta-ethics concerns itself with the nature of moral judgement and asks for example, what are the origins and meanings of ethical principles. Applied ethics deals with major global concepts like capital punishment, abortion, animal rights, and war. Normative ethics is concerned with how people should operate from a moral viewpoint, which also aligns with the orientation of ethics within criminological research as well as research in wider social sciences (Timmons, 2019).

Normative ethics, also known as prescriptive ethics, varies from descriptive ethics, as not only does it not describe how people act, but it also endeavours to tell people how they should act. This is largely done through overarching theories of what constitutes as good, or to act in a righteous manner. Generally, there are three types of normative ethics: virtue ethics, deontology, and consequentialism (Wood, 2020). Each of the three theories can be explored through human action and the three basic dimensions that underpin them. Most human action involves an *agent*, the *act*, and the *consequences*. The three theories that underpin normative ethics at the very least focus on one aspect of human action. Virtue ethics, which will be explored later in this chapter, focusses on the agent and the quest for that person to live a life of moral character. Deontology focusses on the act itself. Finally, consequentialism focusses on the outcome of the consequence (ibid). Deontology and consequentialism share the commonality of asking what is one to do or how should one act.

The central philosophical concept of Kant's deontological work states that there are certain rules, i.e. *categorical imperatives* that are applicable to all people in all places that cannot be violated irrespective of the good that derives from it (Paton, 1971). Taking this logic and applying a criminological example, Kantian ethics would argue that it would be immoral for a person to kill one innocent person even if it meant saving the lives of hundreds, purely on the basis that it is wrong to kill an innocent person. The premise of categorical imperatives is that we all have specific duties that we must adhere to in all scenarios that life presents to us regardless of what the outcome may be. On the contrary, with consequentialism, acts are not intrinsically good or evil. What matters above all is the outcome. A question habitually associated with consequentialism is how we know whether an outcome is good and moral. Often, we determine whether an outcome is positive by assessing if it is beneficial for us. This is known as ethical egoism (Österberg, 1988). On other occasions, we may assess whether the outcome is beneficial only to others, also known as altruistic consequentialism (Portmore, 2020). Yet, the most renowned form of consequentialism that also aligns with classical criminology is utilitarianism. The idea behind utilitarianism is that human action should benefit as many people as possible. This can mean that doing a wrong thing, for example, telling a lie could be a moral act. Both deontology and consequentialism have benefits and limitations.

Deontology offers a universal understanding of certain acts being wrong, irrespective of the situation at hand. It can be viewed as rigid moralism that does not offer flexibility or outcomes for consequences. Returning to the example of lying, some would be comfortable not telling the truth if it meant saving a person's life. Consequentialism, therefore, avoids moral rigidity and is far more pragmatic in complex situations (ibid). With all this in mind, some Western philosophers have an alternative understanding of the ethical responsibility of subjects, which goes against the modern worldview of logical reasoning and clear cut answers. For example, Heidegger's understanding of responsibility differs from the classical modern, Kantian sense (Hofstadter, 1988). Unlike Kant, Heidegger does not view humans in terms of subject, ergo rejecting the thinking of freedom as a form of free will. Derrida, a deconstructivist, who drew inspiration from Heidegger's 'possibility of the impossible', insisted that responsibility is the experience and encounter of a certain im-possible (Epstein, 2019). As stated by Raffoul (2008), Derrida's understanding of the im-possibility of responsibility does not mean something that cannot be, rather it is something that happens beyond the anticipating conditions of possibility of the ecological subject.

Although scholars in the Western world have formalised ethics as a discipline, just like other branches of philosophy, ethics is an active pursuit that is universal. Whether one's thinking is deontological, utilitarian, deconstructivist, or something else, ethics and morality are inextricably linked. Both are concerned with distinguishing the difference between good and bad. Based on our experiences of supervising undergraduate and postgraduate research, as well as sitting on ethics committees, we have observed that most students and academics mainly concern themselves with institutional forms of ethical practice, as opposed to grasping a basic understanding of the philosophies that fortify such practices, as well as their own ethical positionality. It would be unfair to solely pin the blame on researchers, as most research projects, especially in institutional settings, are constrained by time, resources, access, etc. Yet we felt obliged to take an unconventional step by providing a brief understanding of ethics in the previous pages, as this grounding tends to be absent from discussions in research projects as well as the teaching associated with it. In the upcoming chapters, there will be occasions whereby we will refer to certain concepts that align with the ethical practicalities of conducting, dealing with, and managing aspects of qualitative criminological research. Before doing so, it is worthwhile exploring the governance of research ethics and the importance of *reflexivity*.

The Governance of Research Ethics

Irrespective of the criminological area of study, ethics should be at the forefront of any research. The design of qualitative inquiries means that those who conduct research must constantly be mindful of the unpredicted. Social research is a vigorous process of learning that involves intrusion into the lives of those being researched (Wincup, 2017). Social research is therefore contingent upon a successful relationship between the researcher(s) and participant(s). Important to this relationship is the ethical responsibility that is integral to the research topic, design, analysis, and overall project management. The Human Rights Act 1998 and the Data Protection Act 2018, which is the UK's implementation of the General Data Protection Regulation, have both had implications for social research. These two legislations by design have obligated the rights of those involved in research on a statutory footing. Not only do they impact researchers, but they also affect institutions as well as organisations that produce codes of ethics.

Researchers who file for ethical approval are faced with having their proposed work severely scrutinised by ethics committees, with some academics across the world being frustrated with the bureaucracies associated with them. Furedi (2002) expressed concerns about the potential dangers of conducting research because of the obsession that universities have with ethics. He adds that an overly restrictive approach to research will result in a corrosive impact on the exercise of academic freedom. Allen (2008) notes how too often the relationship between research administrators, committee members, and the researcher can result in distrust and conflict. This can subsequently result in researchers being disheartened and halting impactful scholarship (Israel, 2004). However, researchers that can battle through what Haggerty (2004, pp. 392–394) calls 'out of control bureaucracy', may end up abandoning the responsibility of the ethical precepts initially associated with their research because of the boundaries set by an ethics committee.

Irrespective of the frustrations that scholars may have with social research ethics and institutions, ethical procedures adopted by institutions are here to stay. It is vital for readers of this book to understand that the ethical conduct of researchers is a pressing matter of institutional concern because of the degree to which non-cooperation with set standards can expose an entire institution to serious risk. Failure to adhere to institutional rulings can result in serious consequences, for instance being suspended from all research council funding, which is seen to be the pinnacle of research income generation for universities. An example of this is the suspension of all federally financed medical research at Johns Hopkins University in 2001, when a young and healthy volunteer died during a research study. The volunteer, Ellen Roche, died on June 2, 2001, a month after she inhaled an unapproved drug as part of a research study to examine the causes of asthma. Her lungs were destroyed by a chemical that she inhaled. An investigation into Ellen's death revealed that the ethics committee that approved the research had failed to take precise precautions to protect its subjects (Kolata, 2001). Hence, the ethical policing of research by institutions and the scrutiny associated with it should be taken seriously by researchers, to avoid individual and institutional risk. However, researchers should be cognisant of ethics committees influencing research proposals, especially to the detriment of intellectual curiosity that may be shaped because of personal ideologies.

We believe that one of the ways to make sense of all research encounters, from the moment a research idea emerges to when the research ends, is to use a formidable tool known as reflexivity. We deem it to be not only an action of reflection that adds to the credibility of criminological research but also a continuous ethical exercise that holds researchers accountable for their research activities.

Reflexivity as a Continuous Ethical Exercise

If the last century of global criminological scholarship has taught us anything, it is the importance of critical and reflexive thinking. It is an exercise that we have both benefitted from immensely in our own academic careers. Reflexivity is an analytical resource that demands researchers to recognise, evaluate, and take responsibility for one's position within the study and the consequences that their inputs may have on the setting and those being researched, questions being asked, data being generated, and its interpretation. This makes reflexivity a wholesome endeavour and befitting of the interpretive nature of qualitative research. Reflexivity should not be viewed as a mere self-reflection exercise of research events, as both differ in *process*, with the former being a stance that demands the ability to evaluate the influence of oneself within the very act of knowing (research), whereas the latter is to reflect upon the act of knowledge (Popoveniuc, 2014). Within social sciences, reflexivity relates to the object. Research participants by design react to the existence of the researcher, who in turn becomes part of their world. However, the situation is self-reflexive as it involves the researcher's reactions to the behaviour of the studied object (Rahman, 2019). Nagata (2004, p. 139) defines self-reflexivity as 'having an ongoing conversation with your whole self about what you are experiencing as you are experiencing it'. Popoveniuc (2014) argues that reflexivity is an interactive spiral-like stance and process as opposed to a linear one.

In his critical race theory study of black men and their journey towards criminal desistance, Glynn (2014) used reflexivity as a black scholar of race to monitor how his own racial identity impacted his ability to remain objective throughout the course of his study. In doing so, he argued how reflexivity acted as a barometer to identify the ongoing conflict between the subjective and objective aspects of his research. Emirbayer and Desmond's (2012) work on race and reflexivity offers a deeper meaning of scholarly reflexivity, as the authors argue that we must go beyond the understanding that reflexive thinking entails more than how one's social position affects scientific analysis. By utilising Bourdieusian ideas, the authors called for a three-tiered understanding of reflexivity within race scholarship, which to a certain extent can be broadly applied to criminological scholarship. The first concerns *social unconsciousness*, which is the 'occupation of a position in social space and the particular trajectory that has led to it' (Bourdieu, 2000, p. 10). The second concerns the position in *fields* of cultural production, which the authors coin as *disciplinary unconsciousness*. Lastly, the third concerns the *scholastic unconsciousness*, which is the 'invisible determinations inherent in the intellectual posture itself, in the scholarly gaze that [one] casts upon the social world' (Bourdieu & Wacquant, 1992, p. 69). Emirbayer and Desmond (2012, p. 578) posit that the latter two 'have their own internal logic and dynamics, which can profoundly shape what investigators see and fail to see'. The following is a detailed understanding of the two.

The disciplinary unconsciousness requires researchers to explore beyond 'who am I and what my position is within this social setting?'. It demands that one should be able to pragmatically understand the location of the discipline that they are investigating within the wider universe of social sciences. In addition, one should also attempt to understand the self-evident aspect of the studied discipline, which Bourdieu (1977) calls *doxa*. For Bourdieu (2004, p. 94):

> each discipline [has] its own traditional and national particularities, its obligatory problems, its habits of thought, its shared beliefs and self-evidences, its rituals and consecrations, its constraints as regards [to] publication of

findings, its specific forms of censorship, not to mention [a] whole set of presuppositions inscribed in the collective history of the speciality.

(The academic consciousness)

The above offers an understanding of how the researcher can map out the opportunities that are presented within the discipline, which Bourdieu (1996, p. 235) phrases as 'space of possibles'. There is, however, a deconstructivist undertone to consider, which is the space of im-possibles, or in other words, the constraints on discipline innovation. Criminologists occupy different positions within social sciences, as well as engaging differently with the intellectual and scholarly possibles (and im-possibles) that confront them. Naturally, this impacts differences in the work that they produce.

The scholastic unconsciousness is one that holds researchers to account, especially those that have occupied a position within academia for a considerable time. While most criminologists reflect on their positions within social orders, as well as some reflecting on their positionality in disciplines, almost all remain less than fully conscious of how their thinking as scholars carries with it unknown suppositions that distort their perceptions of their research subjects. This aligns with Bourdieu's (2008, p. 23) thinking that 'there are many intellectuals who call the world into question, but very few who call the intellectual world into question'. Scholars, therefore, need to be mindful of the privileges that they occupy (Faheem & Rahman, 2024), and how over time their scientific unconsciousness serves as a disposition that shapes their perception of the social world around them and how they react to it.

While disciplinary and scholastic unconsciousnesses have their own logic and dynamics, they are limited within conventional reflexive understanding, which is to engage in an ongoing practice of pragmatic thinking. Reflexivity is also a philosophical and ethical pursuit. As will be demonstrated through real-life research encounters later, reflexivity is predicated by virtue ethics. The fundamental question in virtue ethics is, 'What should I be?' This is the crucial question that we ask ourselves before embarking on an action. Actions are extremely important as they largely develop us into the person that we want to be. Interestingly, there is a unique relationship between virtue and actions, which is the kind of characteristics that we ought to have, and the kind of actions that we commit. Both are vital for any scholarly engagement, especially primary research. Virtue ethics acknowledges that there is an ethical nature in all activities related to research, not only in ethical dilemmas or during the governance process. It is for this reason that throughout the book, we stress the importance of reflexivity serving as an ethical compass for researchers.

Rationale of the Book and Chapter Summaries

This book has three main components. First, it aims to inform readers and offer practical advice on how they can successfully carry out research and minimise the 'risks' that are often inherent in criminological research. Second, it offers tips and strategies for researchers that might be of use when managing 'boundaries' while conducting criminological research. Lastly, it equips researchers on how to pragmatically deal with 'emotions' when conducting criminological research. These concepts are illustrated primarily through examples we have encountered and documented during our own fieldwork, employing reflexive practice.

This book aims to equip both new and emerging researchers with essential knowledge of research ethics, largely concerning criminological research. While discussing our own experiences in researching topics like gangs, organised crime, criminal exploitation, policing marginalised populations, and homelessness, it draws valuable lessons applicable to various research contexts. It goes beyond a mere methodology text, catering to a wide audience – from students to researchers in both academia and practice. Additionally, it explores the future of ethics in criminological research, offering fresh insights into evolving ethical standards and the importance of adaptation to uphold quality research practices. Given that it provides practical recommendations, this book is also a valuable resource for research stakeholders, including research supervisors, ethics committees, risk-managers, and anyone who is interested in undertaking or teaching research ethics across a broad range of social sciences (criminology, sociology, psychology, law, and education).

To contextualise, Chapter 2 considers the various issues that researchers must consider before pursuing research. It will first consider the notion of inception, which consists of going through an ethics committee process. It then charts key ethical and moral principles that help prevent researchers from being at 'risk' as well as putting those researched at risk. This chapter offers examples, practical advice, and guidance for those pursuing primary research.

Criminological research of qualitative nature often requires the immersion of self within the study in order to establish a personal interaction with research participants, and the environment in which the study is situated. This means the boundaries between the researcher, participants, and research environment(s) can easily become 'blurred'. Therefore, Chapter 3 takes a twofold approach. First, through original and reflexive accounts, it focusses on the issues of boundaries inherent in criminological research. It then offers management tips and strategies for researchers that might be of use when managing such issues.

Chapter 4 extends from the original and reflexive accounts of the previous chapter but draws attention to the emotional labour of conducting criminological research. After the exploration of extant literature, this chapter then considers through novel perspectives how emotions can be managed effectively and then applied to the actual research. Case study examples are offered on key experiences in the field while working with reformed or reforming gang members, and members of organised crime groups who have often opened up emotionally during interviews. In such situations, managing these and the researcher's own emotions become ethical issues, given the need to ensure that no harm (including physical and psychological harm) comes to those participating in the field. The chapter provides illustrations of how emotions are managed during fieldwork, providing essential insights for researchers working with vulnerable and marginalised cohorts.

The final chapter (Chapter 5) summarises the previous chapters of the text. We draw a close to the book by first sharing best practices on how to ethically publish research. We then discuss the future of research ethics in a burgeoning AI world and offer several practical recommendations that can help students, researchers, practitioners, and pracademics to be ethically mindful throughout the course of a research study.

Conclusion

This chapter started by considering philosophy as an active pursuit that we all engage in daily. Philosophical inquiry is the quest to *understand* something rather than to know it. As an active exercise, we *do* philosophy. Philosophers have been around for thousands of years and are dynamic thinkers. Through case and reasoning, they aim to make sense of issues around them and draw conclusions for greater understanding. The etymology of the word, however, as discussed, is concerned with knowledge and one of its branches of knowledge is ethics. Ethics should be viewed as a strand of philosophy that has a direct influence on action. Both philosophy and ethics are intertwined. Philosophy is the study of knowledge, truth, and meaning, whereas ethics often utilises philosophical ideas to explain phenomena. To be a moral citizen in this world, we need to know our position and responsibilities. It is for this reason that we felt the need to offer an abstract understanding of normative ethics so that readers can make sense of the core tenets before applying it within the context of research.

Philosophical ideologies, like any other form of knowledge, should not be taken at face value. We encourage readers to challenge and contest them. After all, they often serve as guidelines and boundaries that keep us on track. They become part of our disposition and have implications for our moral beliefs. In a world that is dominated by fake news and cancel culture, humans have become susceptible to being misinformed. Therefore, philosophy and all that it entails allows us to challenge our own worldly views. Ethics in social research is often viewed as an administrative process that is a tick box exercise filled with institutional bureaucracy. While we are aware of the governance associated with it, we believe that ethics should be the backbone of any research-related activity. Researchers need to be mindful of the implications that research activities have for them, the institution(s) that they represent and wider society. Overcoming bureaucratic ethical obstacles is a valuable accountability exercise that can help build researcher credibility, research integrity, and public support for community based scholarly work. In addition, many of the ethical norms in research promote other important moral and social values, such as social responsibility, compliance with law, human rights, public health, and safety. While ethics committees are adamant that all potential research-related risks need to be addressed prior to the approval of a project, we need to anticipate the inevitability of the unexpected, i.e. the im-possibles of the discipline (Raffoul, 2008). In this chapter, we introduced the importance of reflexivity and the value that it offers to researchers. We view it as a continuous ethical exercise because if carried out correctly, it traverses across all research endeavours, and its links with ontology and epistemology enable us to integrate ethical, social, and political judgements of the research journey, therefore increasing the accountability for the knowledge that is produced. At a basic level, reflexivity allows us to connect with ourselves and those around us, the standpoint from which we speak, and the social and political context in which interactions take place. If practised at a deeper level, we can attain an awareness of how traditions within our discipline can influence what constitutes knowledge and the way research is carried out. We offer examples of our own reflexivity throughout the book, and we begin by doing this in the next chapter, which considers research inception and dealing with the 'risks' associated with qualitative criminological research.

References

Allen, G. (2008) Getting beyond form filling: The role of institutional governance in human research ethics. *Journal of Academic Ethics*, 6(2), 105–116.

Bilge, S. (2013) Intersectionality undone: Saving intersectionality from feminist intersectionality. *Du Bois Review: Social Science Research on Race*, 10(2), 405–424.

Bourdieu, P. (1977) *Outline of a theory of practice*. Cambridge: Cambridge University Press.

Bourdieu, P. (1996) *The rules of art: Genesis and structure of the literary field*. Stanford, CA: Stanford University Press.

Bourdieu, P. (2000) *Pascalian meditations*. Stanford, CA: Stanford University Press.

Bourdieu, P. (2004) *Science of science and reflexivity*. Chicago, IL: University of Chicago.

Bourdieu, P. (2008) *Sketch for a self-analysis*. Chicago, IL: University of Chicago Press.

Bourdieu, P., & Wacquant, L. J. D. (1992) *An invitation to reflexive sociology*. Chicago, IL: University of Chicago Press.

Carbin, M., & Edenheim, S. (2013) The intersectional turn in feminist theory: A dream of a common language?. *European Journal of Women's Studies*, 20(3), 233–248.

Chalmers, D. J. (1996) *The conscious mind: In search of a fundamental theory*. New York: Oxford University Press.

Crenshaw, K. (1989) Demarginalizing the intersection of race and sex: A black feminist critique of antidiscrimination doctrine, feminist theory and antiracist politics. *University of Chicago Legal Forum*, 8, 139–167

Data Protection Act (2018) Available at: <https://www.legislation.gov.uk/ukpga/2018/12/contents/enacted>. Last accessed: 11 September 2022.

Deigh, J. (2010) *An introduction to ethics.* New York: Cambridge University Press.

Emirbayer, M., & Desmond, M. (2012) Race and reflexivity. *Ethnic and Racial Studies,* 35(4), 574–599.

Epstein, M. (2019) *A philosophy of the possible: Modalities in thought and culture.* Leiden: Koninklijke.

Faheem, A., & Rahman, M. (2024). "Never let anyone tell you that you're not good enough": Using intersectionality to reflect on inequality in British academia. In M. Islam & A. Mahmud (eds.), *Uncovering Islamophobia in higher education: Supporting the success of Muslim students and staff.* London: Palgrave Macmillan.

Furedi, F. (2002) Don't rock the research boat. Available at: <https://www.timeshigher education.com/news/dont-rock-the-research-boat/166585.article>. Last accessed: 11 September 2022.

Glynn, M. (2014) *Black men, invisibility and crime: Towards a critical race theory of desistance.* London: Routledge.

Haggerty, K. D. (2004) Ethics creep: Governing social science research in the name of ethics. *Qualitative Sociology,* 27(4), 391–414.

Hofstadter, A. (1988)*The basic problems of phenomenology.* Bloomington: Indiana University Press.

Human Rights Act (1998) Available at: <https://www.legislation.gov.uk/ukpga/1998/42/contents>. Last accessed: 11 September 2022.

Israel, M. (2004) *Ethics and the governance of criminological research in Australia.* Sydney: Report for the New South Wales Bureau of Crime Statistics and Research.

Jibrin, R., & Salem, S. (2015) Revisiting intersectionality: Reflections on theory and praxis. *Transcripts: An Interdisciplinary Journal in the Humanities and Sciences,* 5, 7–24.

Kolata, G. (2001) Johns Hopkins death brings halt to U.S.-financed human studies. Available at: <https://www.nytimes.com/2001/07/20/us/johns-hopkins-death-brings-halt-to-us-financed-human-studies.html>. Last accessed: 11 September 2022.

Nagata, A. L. (2004) Promoting self-reflexivity in intercultural education. *Journal of Intercultural Communication,* 8, 139–167.

Österberg, J. (1988) *Self and others: A study of ethical egoism.* Dordrecht: Kluwer Academic Publishers.

Paton, H. J. (1971) *The categorical imperative: A study in Kant's moral philosophy.* PA: University of Pennsylvania Press.

Popoveniuc, B. (2014) Self-reflexivity: The ultimate end of knowledge. *Procedia Social and Behavioral Sciences,* 163, 204–213.

Portmore, D. W. (2020) *The oxford handbook of consequentialism.* New York: Oxford University Press.

Poulton, R. (2019) *The little book of philosophy.* London: Summersdale.

Poulton, R. (2021) *The little book of philosophy.* Chichester: Summersdale.

Raffoul, F. (2008) Derrida and the ethics of the im-possible. *Research in Phenomenology,* 38(2), 270–290.

Rahman, M. (2019) *Homicide and organised crime: Ethnographic narratives of serious violence in the criminal underworld.* London: Palgrave.

Timmons, M. (2019) *Oxford studies in normative ethics* (9th edition). London: Oxford University Press.

Wincup, E. (2017) *Criminological research: Understanding qualitative methods* (2nd edition). London: Sage.

Wood, N. (2020) *Virtue rediscovered: Deontology, consequentialism, and virtue ethics in the contemporary moral landscape.* London: Rowman & Littlefield.

2 Dealing with Risks

Applying for Ethical Approval and Changes after Ethical Approval

Introduction

Applying for Ethical Approval

In Chapter 1, we discussed some of the different theories that underpin ethics as a philosophy. This chapter offers the pragmatics of ethics within criminological research. In their statement of ethics, The British Society of Criminology (2015) stresses the importance of undertaking research through rigorous methodology, so as to be able to achieve the highest quality of scholarship in order to maximise knowledge and benefits accrued to society. To do this, researchers are required to apply for ethical approval for any research that they wish to undertake.

Most universities will have at the very least a faculty-level ethics committee. Some may have department or subject-level committees. An ethics committee consists of a group of appointed people, usually a mixture of academic and professional staff that will be trained to formally assess if the proposed research is 'ethical'. Usually, they are given a set amount of time to review and offer feedback before approval or rejection of an application. To avoid the delay in reviewing an application, an applicant should strive to offer extensive attention to the proposed research through focussed research aims and objectives. Gaining ethical approval should not be viewed as a tick-box exercise that is detached from the overall research; rather, it should be viewed as part of the research design process. Here, it is important to note that an ethics application for criminological research may be reviewed by a committee member whose primary expertise may fall within the remit of other social sciences (e.g. sociology, psychology, political science, etc.). Hence, incorporating ethical considerations into the research design process enables researchers to reflect on potential physical and psychological risks, while also facilitating reviewers from diverse academic backgrounds to provide a thorough risk assessment.

The application for ethical approval will vary across institutions. Yet all applications will have a core list of questions that applicants will need to address to determine the viability of the project. While institutions will

DOI: 10.4324/9781003304746-2

provide guidance to applicants that will aid the completion of the application, in the next few sections, we offer an understanding of prevalent questions that we have come across when applying for research ethics.

Prevalent Ethical Questions

Prior to engaging in semi-structured questions in the application, applicants are likely to encounter several screening questions. This initial line of questioning serves the fundamental purpose of ascertaining the degree of inherent 'risk' intrinsic to the project under consideration. These inquiries necessitate the provision of detailed information concerning several facets, including but not limited to the involvement of human subjects, animals, or other forms of wildlife in the data collection process, the potential for data analysis to disclose individual identities, the exploration of sensitive subjects such as terrorism or extremism, or the requisition of governmental clearances for project execution. While the perception of risk may differ from that of the applicant to those reviewing the application, we think that ethics committees' assessment of risk at universities determines the scrutiny associated with the project. It is our contention that the determination of risk by ethics committees operating within academic institutions fundamentally informs the level of scrutiny associated with the proposed project.

Within the remit of one of our institutional paradigms, if a prospective research project is adjudged to carry a high-risk quotient, the application would be subjected to further examination by a specialised committee comprising several academics. This dedicated committee would engage in extensive deliberations pertaining to the application's merits and drawbacks before making a final decision. Moreover, it is incumbent upon applicants to respond to additional screening queries pertaining to their own safety and that of their research subjects. For instance, certain scholars have embarked upon ethnographic studies involving criminological subjects, a context that may entail solo research endeavours in unfamiliar or isolated locales and cultures. While such scholarship is impressive for its rigour, it concurrently produces a nexus of safeguarding considerations for the researcher and those researched.

Further safeguarding inquiries are pertinent to this discourse and encompass various dimensions. Notably, these inquiries encompass the age categorisation of research participants, particularly ascertaining whether they fall below the age of 18 or qualify as vulnerable adults. Additionally, the screening process seeks to recognise if the act of posing research-related questions could inadvertently lead to breaches of confidentiality or the revelation of illicit activities and behaviours on the part of participants.

Most ethics applications will require the input of basic project information. This largely involves details of the research team, the title of the project, research aims, and objectives. Given that all projects have a timeframe, applicants will be required to provide a start and end date of the proposed research.

Offering a realistic timeframe is crucial. If fieldwork continues beyond the provided end date, an amended application may need to be submitted to the committee. The reviewer, or the ethics committee, will be interested in a brief outline of the project. Here, they will seek to understand the justification of the research and the potential benefits to the wider population. Any response should be clear, and defining subject-specific terms is important as the reviewer may not be familiar with key terminology. When offering context, an applicant can refer to existing research that is relevant to their project. Not only is this good academic practice – dare we say ethical too – but it is also helpful for the reviewer to appreciate the relevance of the research and its contribution towards society. To understand the ethical dimensions of your project, reviewers will extensively focus on where primary data will be collected, what collection methods will be used, and why. Data can be sourced on online forums (e.g. using a university-approved survey website, social media platforms, etc), or in person (e.g. in university campus space, community settings, schools, etc). Offering specific information about data sites is imperative as it helps reviewers assess the potential risks of the research from an environmental standpoint.

Recruitment of Participants and Data Collection

The process of recruiting participants needs to be clearly stipulated and acknowledgement must be made that there is no obligation to take part (see below section *Supporting Documents* for further information). Recruiting participants can pose challenges, particularly for students and junior academics. In some cases, researchers may conduct participant recruitment based on predefined inclusion and exclusion criteria. To illustrate, Rahman and Abdulkader's (2022, p. 26) research delved into the factors that make rough sleepers vulnerable and susceptible to victimisation. This research employed purposive sampling and therefore had a specific inclusion and exclusion criteria. Consequently, participants for the study were sourced from a homeless charity organisation. The following extract from their study provides insights into how collaboration with stakeholders can help address ethical concerns during participant recruitment.

> we engaged proactively with the outreach service coordinator of the organisation to further understand the complexities of rough sleepers. On reflection, this exercise served us well, as we took a more ethical, mindful and compassionate approach to certain aspects of the research process, as well as caution during all primary investigations.
>
> Given the nature of those under investigation, this study took a purposive sampling approach. This sampling approach, like all sampling approaches, has its limitations. For instance, some have considered it to be extremely

prone to researcher bias (Burnard, 2011). However, as researchers, we took a non-judgmental approach to the study, and as alluded to above, dialogue between the service coordinator before the primary investigations as well as continuous individual reflexivity helped reduce any biases. Purposive sampling has also been accused of being susceptible to data manipulation, as those selected for the project could initiate change in their behaviour (Emmel, 2013). To mitigate this risk, it was agreed with the community partner and signed off by the chief executive that all primary investigations with rough sleepers would include the presence of their caseworkers. Based on their expertise and rapport with participants, caseworkers were best positioned to make a judgement on any data manipulation.

This study was interested in speaking to individuals who were once, or still are rough sleepers, that have either felt vulnerable or criminally victimised, or have observed other rough sleepers feeling vulnerable or criminally victimised. As such, one of the major benefits of purposive sampling was the ability to target niche demographics to obtain specific data points (Burnard, 2011). Another strength of purposive sampling is that it allows researchers to study those that are knowledgeable about the issues under investigation (Polit & Beck, 2009). Hence, the community partner carefully identified suitable participants that would be able to offer insight into their lived experiences.

The passage above suggests the importance of authors engaging in reflexivity, a process that aids in recognising and addressing personal biases. For the authors, this practice served as a safeguard against potential criticism for employing what may be perceived as a manipulative sampling method. Moreover, involving stakeholders in the data collection process enabled the researchers to enhance their ability to mitigate inherent risks associated with working with a vulnerable population, which is something that the ethics committee would have been mindful of prior to approving the research.

Outlining the desired data collection method (e.g. ethnography, interviews, focus groups, observation, archival, etc.) in an ethics application form may seem irrelevant and somewhat intrusive. However, given the various ways that criminological data can be collected, and the interactions associated with them, applicants will be required to provide a clear rationale for their choice and an explanation as to why the method is best suited for their research. To offer a persuasive argument for this section, attention can be drawn to existing research that has utilised similar data collection methods. Below is the response given by Rahman and Abdulkader in their ethics application on data collection.

After several informal conversations with charity managers who work closely with homeless people, I have been made aware that focus group discussions (FGDs) are often used when working with homeless people. In social research, FGD embraces a range of different procedures, but the common denominator is that participants are allowed to engage with each other voluntarily within an ethical setting. In addition, FGDs have been successfully used for previous research on homelessness (Stoecker, 2001; Fujimura, 2003; Cheng & Kumar, 2012). Given that this research also explores the 'affective dimensions' of homeless individuals (i.e. their moods, attitudes, and motivations), FGDs as a method helps appreciate how people think and feel about an experience, issue, or service.

All FGDs will be audio-recorded and transcribed by the principal investigator. Upon transcription, all of the audio recordings will be deleted. Of note, the questions in the 'interview schedule' have been formulated to be able to achieve the research aim/objectives as well as considering previous research that has been done on homelessness (Stoecker, 2001; Cheng & Kumar, 2012). Hence, the research question is appropriate for the target audience.

(Application reference: Rahman/4993/R(B)/2020/Mar/ BLSS)

The above example serves to substantiate the significance of employing focus group discussions as a methodological approach in the investigation of homelessness, as evidenced by extant scholarly literature. Furthermore, it tangentially alludes to its practical viability as an investigative instrument, stemming from dialogues held with charity managers. Hence, it is imperative not only to establish the ethical soundness of the chosen data collection method but also to underscore its capacity as a credible means of procuring primary data. Of note, in instances where multiple data collection methods are employed or the research project involves distinct cohorts of participants, it is essential upon the applicant to provide full disclosure of these methodologies and elucidate the rationale underpinning their selection.

Anonymity and Confidentiality

Upholding anonymity and confidentiality is a key ethical precept, and both need to be considered in detail when applying for ethical approval. Anonymity is when there is no knowledge of the personal data of research participants. As such, even the researcher is unable to trace any identifiable information of the participants. This is often the case in quantitative studies where survey-based research is conducted with structured questions. Confidentiality is when researchers are privy to the personal data of participants, but this information is not revealed to those outside of the study. The process of confidentiality is mainly required in qualitative studies, where interviews, focus groups, ethnography, and other face-to-face approaches are employed to generate data. In some instances, both anonymity and confidentiality may not be guaranteed. This can be either a result of the nature of the research or professional regulatory statutory body (PRSB) requirements regarding safeguarding. If this is the case for applicants, any breach of anonymity or confidentiality must be justified so that the committee is aware that the applicant is mindful of these issues.

Data Storage, Transfer, and Destruction

Part of maintaining anonymity and confidentiality is the storage, transferring, and destruction of research data. In the UK, the EU General Data Protection Regulation (GDPR) and the UK Data Protection Act 2018 govern the processing (acquiring, holding, using, etc.) of personal data in the UK. While the legislation has not been specifically designed for research, it is still viewed as the governance to use for lawful, fair, and transparent data processing. For applicants working with electronic data, they will need to specify how this type of data will be handled. From our experiences, we have stored electronic data (e.g. digital copies of interview schedules, participant information sheets, consent forms, debrief sheets, transcripts, etc.) in our institutional digital devices that are encrypted and password protected. Further to this, we tend to transfer our data to our institutional servers and when erasing research data, we follow the guidance that has been set out by our IT departments. As for physical data (e.g. paper-based copies of interview schedules, participant information sheets, consent forms, debrief sheets, transcripts, etc.), we store such data in locked drawers or cabinets located in our institutions. Any data that we need to transfer from one location to another is done by a private mode of transport. When destroying physical copies, we do so by using confidential waste facilities that are provided by our institutions. The storage, transfer, and destruction of research data invariably differs across institutions, and therefore applicants should refer to any guidance information in relation to this or contact a member of the ethics committee prior to submitting their application.

Supporting Documents

Supporting documents are key research instruments that are outward facing artefacts that applicants need to provide to those who will partake in the research. The three main supporting documents that researchers should provide participants are:

1. *Participant information sheet*

A participant information sheet is a document that should consist of enough accessible information so that participants can decide as to whether they consent to the research. The language of the document should be accessible and appropriate to the intended. A participant information sheet usually consists of the following information:

- *Title of the study:* For consistency, the study title should be the exact title on the ethics application.
- *Aims and objectives of the study:* Clear aims and objectives need to be offered.
- *A brief explanation as to why the participant has been chosen to partake in the study:* An example of this could be that they have the general knowledge base or a particular set of expertise, or are part of a cohort that the research has an extensive focus on.
- *Whether participation is voluntary:* In some cases, participation in a study may be mandatory (e.g., a child's participation in a pedagogical or criminal intervention). Therefore, it needs to be made clear in this document that consent is required to use the data from the intervention as part of the study (this also needs to be made clear in the ethics application form). If the participation is voluntary, it needs to be made clear that non-participation is an option and will not have any adverse effects on their access to services, education, or safety.
- *Expectations from participants as a researcher:* Here, an applicant needs to be mindful of time, i.e. how much time, how frequently, and for how long the participation will involve. For students and junior academics, our advice would be for applicants to talk with the wider research team or an experienced researcher when ascertaining the duration of research encounters.
- *Potential benefits of participating:* In some cases, research participation may result in financial compensation to reimburse participants for their time or expenses. Participation may also contribute to the influence of policy or practice change. These will need to be acknowledged where relevant.
- *Potential risk of participating:* On this point, an applicant needs to reflect on the risk of participants providing commentary on aspects of their own beliefs, values, ideologies, and perspectives in relation to criminological matters.
- *Confidentiality arrangements:* This is a crucial section of the documentation as the applicant needs to have arrangements in place to protect identity and anonymity. If the study requires the use of media for data collection (e.g. photos and videos), there needs to be an acknowledgement of how confidentiality will be maintained. Upholding participant confidentiality should be a concern from the inception of the study, data collection, data storage, data analysis, and write-up.

- *Participants rights:* An explanation should be offered that participants have the right to informed consent, the right to withdraw from the study at any stage (without any consequences), the right to anonymity, confidentiality, and data protection.
- *Who are the funders?* Details for research that is being funded (e.g. a postgraduate scholarship or research grant) should be provided. This will not apply to all studies.
- *Details of the research and further contact information:* For research transparency and accountability, information needs to be offered so that the applicant and their organisation can be contacted in the future (e.g. full name, email addresses, telephone numbers).

2. *Consent form*

A consent form is a signed and dated document that evidences participant consent. The document should be structured so that participants can comfortably agree to each facet of the study. If participants vary across the study, the applicant should create a separate form. Those who engage in a research study will need to provide consent and therefore need to have the capacity to do so. If a participant lacks the capacity to do so (e.g. they are under the age of 16, are mentally unstable, or cannot read and write), sufficient measures will need to be put in place for the researcher to achieve consent. A consent form should consist of the following information:

- *Title of the study:* For consistency, the study title should be the exact title in the ethics application and what is written in the participant information sheet.
- *A brief overview of the topic:* By the time participants go through the consent form, they should have sufficient knowledge of the study. However, this document can refer to the aims and objectives of the study.
- *A brief statement about voluntary participation:* It is crucial that the document has explicit information about what aspects of the study are voluntary and this information should resonate with what has been mentioned in the participant information sheet. If the study requires mandatory participation, this will also need to be considered in the consent form.
- *Opportunity for participants to indicate consent:* Participants can signify their consent by ticking boxes to indicate:
    - That they understand the study and have understood any other information that has been presented to them.
    - That they understand that participation is voluntary.
    - That they have had the opportunity to ask any questions.

- That they agree to take part and therefore agree to be interviewed, audio recorded, video recorded, or whatever may be relevant ethically to capture data.
- That they understand the right to withdraw from the study without any consequences. An explanation will need to be given of what will happen to participant data if they withdraw and up to what point they can withdraw. For example, with survey and focus group-based research, it may be difficult to pinpoint individual research data.
- They understand that any information provided by them may be used for outputs while maintaining anonymity and confidentiality.

3. *Debrief sheet*

A debrief sheet needs to offer participants details of the next steps of the study once their participation comes to an end. Ethically, participants have a right to know the future of the study. This document can provide information that reiterates the importance of partaking in the study and details of the researcher if participants want updates on the progress of the research. Additionally, it should offer contact information of professional organisations that can support participants if they experience any form of distress. Providing this referral information is essential as researchers have the ethical responsibility to mitigate any physical or psychological risks that are research based. Lastly, there should be information on the document as to whom to contact to log a complaint. This should either be the chair of the relevant ethics committee for research related matters or the data protection officer if the complaint relates to data protection.

Access Request Letter

Before research can commence, a researcher may need to get access to an organisation, resources, data, or even potential participants. Therefore, permission of access will need to be achieved, which is often done by seeking access from a person that has the authorisation to give access. For example, if an applicant is interested in researching homelessness and is keen on acquiring a practitioner's perspective, they would ideally need to get permission for access from management. An access request letter is similar to that of a Participant Information Sheet; however, instead of offering information to potential participants, the purpose is to inform a stakeholder about the project to obtain permission for access.

The letter should be addressed to the individual from whom access is being requested, and it should clearly include all relevant information in relation to the study. Here, it is important to note that the access request letter is a preview of what you intend to send to seek permission of access upon the ethical approval of your study, as opposed to what is sent prior to seeking ethical approval. Therefore, an access request letter is viewed favourably by a research ethics committee as it serves as transparent evidence of the future communication between the applicant and those whom they intend to engage with.

Changes after Ethical Approval

It is important for researchers to be aware of significant changes that may occur in their study upon ethical approval. This is something that can be monitored through reflexivity, where researchers can diarise on a regular basis to establish shifts in their work. As researchers, we have experienced significant changes in the methodological aspects in some of our projects from what we initially planned. Significant changes include employing a new research method or modifying an existing one. They may result in the engagement of a new group of participants, a different participant recruitment method, a different approach to giving information to participants (e.g. changing how consent is given for the study), a different method of data collection, and a different location to collect data. If change occurs, the researcher will then need to contact the ethics administrator of the committee and will need to adhere to the process of making changes, which may result in the amendment of the approved application or the submission of a new application. Below are some illustrative examples of methodological changes that required ethical adjustments.

Illustrative Example 1: Ethnography: Using Ethnographic Principles to Carry Out Technology-Facilitated Research [Source: Rahman 2016; Rahman 2019]

Rahman (2019) investigated the causes of serious violence related to organised crime in the West Midlands, England. This research stemmed from his doctoral study conducted between 2014 and 2017, using ethnographic and case study methodologies. During this research, Rahman (2016) also published a conference proceeding based on one of the cases. Throughout the doctoral study and the related publications, participants were observed using traditional ethnographic methods. This involved observing them in different social settings and recording detailed fieldnotes. The primary function of ethnography is to draw upon a wide range of sources to make a systematic sense of people and cultures in their natural state. This means that a key element of ethnography is a detailed exploration of the social world within its natural setting, as opposed to those created artificially or imposed environments as found with surveys and experiments. Advocates of this method have persuasively argued it to be a holistic approach to research, as ethnographers draw upon a swathe of information sources such as: documentaries, secondary data, archived information, in-depth interviews, case studies, in addition to what

Armstrong (1993, p. 7) describes as 'going out amongst the research subjects' to undertake direct comprehensive observations.

Critics of this approach to research have argued data reliability, validity, and generalisability. They have also questioned the lack of standardised procedures that are often prevalent in positivist approaches (Bryman, 2016). The main criticism of ethnography is that it produces subjective findings and idiosyncratic impressions that cannot offer a meaningful foundation for rigorous scientific analysis (Marcus, 2021). However, Gunter (2010) argues that what tends to be overlooked in debates between positivists and naturalists are the intra-ethnographic disputes around 'realism' and 'relativism'. Some will view the aim of ethnography is to 'discover and represent faithfully the true nature of social phenomena' (Hammersley, 1992, p. 44), which automatically ignores the impact that researchers may have upon the collection and interpretation of social facts. On the contrary, others argue the 'social and historical constraints on what can be claimed as the truth' (Scheurich, 1997, p. 34), therefore suggesting that social words and supposed 'realities' are mere 'constructs'. Ultimately, through the interactions that they partake in, ethnographers contribute to existing social worlds, as opposed to just ethically capturing the truthful essence of a social phenomenon. Important here is to note that it is possible to cut through many of the above discourses about the limitations and strengths of ethnography by placing reflexivity at the forefront of social research. Litcherman (2016, p. 35) states that 'since interpretations are part of explanation in much ethnography, interpretive reflexivity widens our ability to assess causal as well as interpretive claims', thus as noted below (Rahman, 2019, p. 9), it considers social positions within ongoing circuits of communication between researcher and researched.

> I could overtly observe social interactions as they organically occurred. In doing so, as an 'outsider', I benefitted from gaining insider understanding of people involved in criminal activities or indeed of those who are involved in responding to criminal activities.

During fieldwork, Rahman investigated case studies of homicide that were motivated by organised crime related activities. Part of the fieldwork required visiting the locations where the homicides took place, as it served as a sense-making exercise to determine the flow of life around a location as people go about their day-to-day activities, as opposed to the abstracted snapshots that reports of a homicide represent. In criminology, this is known as a 'criminological autopsy'. Further to this, locations were also visited to systematically observe the landscape and to compare it to how it was when the homicides took place based on what was published by newspapers and court recordings. However, once it was established during the early stages of the fieldwork that some of the participants in the study had extensive knowledge about the location of the homicides, the street-level ethnography and the observations associated with them changed. The triangulation of participant knowledge, access to court data, as well as information from news outlets meant significant data collection changes. As such, Rahman utilised his car and dash-cam video technology within it to conduct and capture ethnographic data beyond the conventional approach. Given that most cases of homicide that he investigated involved the use of a car or took place in outdoor spaces, he would drive to the crime scenes with a willing and knowledgeable research participant. The reflexive excerpt below reveals how this proved to be an unconventional yet useful method of collecting observation-based data.

> First, the dash-cam ethnography process becomes a reconstruction of events, which therefore allows researchers from 'outsider' perspectives to make sense of places and spaces that are essential for the crime under investigation. In addition, this provides the potential to identify additional places and spaces that may be of significance. Second, as the process is essentially a journey of space, if the researcher is accompanied by a participant, then there is a likelihood of narratives emerging about spaces that are socially, culturally, economically or criminally significant to the participant. In turn, this may prove to be beneficial for the researcher when analysing the overarching factors of his or her subject. Third, the process can have an impact on emotions and recollections, and this may also prove to be crucial for the trajectory of participant narratives and lived experiences. Finally, as the journey is recorded visually, the researcher does not have the burden of recollecting the ethnographic encounter once it is finished and has the luxury of replaying the footage. In short, the points above identify how an innovative method can help the collation, interpretation, and analysis of criminological data.
>
> (Researcher's fieldnotes, adapted from Rahman, 2019)

'TECHNOLOGY-FACILITATED RESEARCH' REFLECTIONS BY RAHMAN

The above examples offer an understanding of how technological developments can alter the way that an ethnographic inquiry is carried out. While detailed notes are still a mainstay of ethnographic fieldwork, the capturing of rich narratives without any omissions in video and audio formats augments the conventional approach and serves as a vital tool that extensively facilitates an in-depth investigation of a crime through the observation of environments, peoples, and cultures. Important here is to recognise the ethical dimensions of carrying out an ethnographic inquiry through the extensive use of technology or a vehicle. Ethical approval was granted by my institution to carry out ethnography by adopting a traditional approach. However, when it was decided during the early stages of the fieldwork that the approach to conduct ethnographic research would involve the use of a vehicle and recording technology, I was required to revise the initial ethics application.

A key mandate of a research ethics committee is to protect the rights, dignity, safety, and well-being of people that participate in research. This includes the researcher, those that are researched and the communities where research activities take place. For these reasons, when I was required to revise my ethics application, I needed to provide justifications about the strengths and limitations for taking a more innovative approach while retaining the fundamentals of the method. I was also required to reevaluate the feasibility of the study and the practicalities of using a vehicle for recorded research activities – i.e. a risk assessment of using a vehicle for carrying out research, maintenance of the vehicle, petrol costs, the dash-cam set-up, and the transfer and storage of recorded data.

Illustrative Example 2: Data Collection during COVID-19: From the Analogue World to the Digital [Source: Rahman & Abdulkader 2022]

In some instances, changes in a research project are beyond the control of the researcher. This was the case for scholars around the world during the coronavirus 2019 (COVID-19) pandemic. While some studies reveal that COVID-19 resulted in an influx of publications (Harper et al., 2020), a survey by UK Research and Innovation (2021) revealed that 61% of researchers reported lockdown or shielding had negatively impacted their time for research. Also in the survey, 27% agreed COVID-19 had provided unexpected opportunities for their research. Thankfully, the latter was also the case for Rahman and Abdulkader (2022), who took a purposive sampling research approach to explore the precursors that result in homeless people feeling vulnerable and subsequently victimised. The initial methodological approach prior to the first COVID-19 lockdown consisted of a focus group discussion and a one-to-one follow-up semi-structured interview with each participant. To achieve research focus as well as accomplish the aim of the project, the original idea was to code the data generated from the focus group prior to holding semi-structured interviews with each participant. The focus group discussion took place one week before the first UK lockdown in March 2020. This meant that there was no time to carry out the individual interviews in person.

'FROM THE ANALOGUE WORLD TO THE DIGITAL' REFLECTIONS BY RAHMAN

It would be naïve for researchers to assume that the transition to carry out research activity online, which was intended to take place in person, is a seamless task. The pandemic has transformed research methods and has made it appealing to carry out certain activities online. However, the convenience of conducting research online does not mean that ethical considerations should be downplayed. For me and Maram, the change in collecting data from in person to online required our approved ethics application to be amended. The amended application focussed on four key aspects:

1. **Appropriateness and possible risks:** As the principal investigator of the project, I spent a period carefully reviewing if the research topic was appropriate for online interviews, or if it posed a risk for those involved. For example, given that our study explored aspects of victimisation concerning rough sleepers, I first assessed the sensitivity of what could potentially be discussed. This allowed me to consider the implications of participant well-being during and after the interview.

2. **Interview consent:** In most instances, research participants should receive a physical copy of the Participant Information Sheet prior to the interview to sign and date. Online interviews require consent to be obtained via email. Given that our interviews of rough sleepers were facilitated by a charity, they sent the consent forms to the caseworkers assigned to each rough sleeper. For best practice, they also verbally re-confirmed informed consent for participation before commencing each interview.

3. **Confidentiality:** To uphold confidentiality throughout interviews, I extensively explored technological and logistical aspects to ensure that they and their interviewees had privacy on their devices. They also considered the environments where dialogues would take place. For them, this required all interviews to take place in a quiet and private location where digital screens cannot be seen by others. When it was time to interview, we encouraged the use of headphones rather than computer speakers to reduce the likelihood of interactions being overheard. As noted, given that the interviews were facilitated by a charity, the devices that were used by the interviewees were the laptops of their caseworkers, and the location that they participated in was in one of the buildings owned by the charity. Along with upholding confidentiality, this also helped the data management of conducting online interviews.

4. **Data Management:** Along with conventional data management considerations, we were both concerned about where interview recordings would be stored. The online communication platform licences that organisations are subscribed to vary. Due to institution policy, we were only allowed to use Microsoft Teams. Some of the alternatives to Microsoft Teams currently are Zoom, Google Chat, Slack, and Webex Suite. As such, it is imperative for researchers to be aware of what platforms they can use, whether they are research-friendly, and whether access to the same platform can be achieved for the interviewees. Researchers also need to be mindful of the recording features of the platform they use as well as the potential use of an alternative recording device as a backup. For our study, we both interviewed each participant on separate devices remotely in a private location. All the interviews were recorded and

saved on Microsoft Teams. At the end of each interview, the recordings were uploaded on Microsoft OneDrive.

The illustrative examples offered in this chapter demonstrate that research methodologies can change because of innovative practice or unforeseen circumstances. Researchers, therefore, should not be fixated on one approach and should be open to the idea that changes may occur, especially if a project involves human participation. The examples have highlighted how technology can serve as a means for acquiring data. It also revealed how researchers maximise resources at their disposal when change is necessary. For example, Rahman and Abdulkader (2022, p. 26) were able to successfully work with a vulnerable cohort online by involving a professional who had a working relationship with the research participants. By working with this professional, they were able to:

> further understand the complexities of rough sleepers. On reflection, this exercise served us well, as we took a more ethical, mindful and compassionate approach to certain aspects of the research process, as well as caution during all primary investigations.

Most decisions made by researchers have ethical consequences that can be unpacked conceptually through a reflexive orientation known as 'methodological reflexivity' (Olmos-Vega et al., 2022). Walsh (2003) views this to be a practice that helps researchers critically consider the nuances and impacts of their methodological decisions by offering thoughtful consideration of their paradigmatic orientation(s). Finlay (2002) argues that any form of reflexivity is tied to a researcher's capability to make and communicate nuanced ethical decisions amid the complex work of generating real-world data that reflects participant experiences and social practices. Varpio et al. (2020) acknowledge the complexities of acquiring primary research data and argue that methodological decision-making should not be set at the beginning of a research process; rather, reflexive researchers should constantly make decisions or react appropriately to unforeseen circumstances. The commentary offered by the scholars above reinforces our standpoint in Chapter 1, which argues that reflexivity is a continuous ethical practice. If this is practised correctly and consistently by researchers, like the illustrations in this chapter, it will enable them to make decisions that are ethical, rigorous, and paradigmatically aligned.

Of note, obtaining ethical approval for research endeavours and maintaining ongoing reflexivity, while crucial, does not guarantee complete mitigation of potential risks for both researchers and participants. Instead, we contend that such measures serve to alleviate potential risks. Consequently, an appreciation of risk theory is important to facilitate informed decision-making by researchers engaged in sensitive research pursuits.

Risks for Researchers and Participants

One of the most fundamental properties of human behaviour is risk aversion (Zhang et al., 2014). This has made the monitoring of risk by humans a key aspect of contemporary society (Beck, 1992; Giddens, 1991). Beck's (1992, p. 5) work on risk society argues that risks 'only exist in terms of the (scientific or anti-scientific) knowledge'. By this, Beck alluded to the fact that the understanding of risk is an emotive and subjective concept that can be altered, amplified, dramatised, or minimised based on knowledge. The assessment of risk in everyday life plays into the formation of how the social world is configured. Fox (1998) notes that existing and functioning in a risk-based society encourages us to be more self-reflexive, which allows us to appreciate the hazards that impact our everyday activities. Lupton (2002) further argues that examining daily practices encourages reflexivity, accountability, and responsibility. Given that we can minimise risk through knowledge (Beck, 1992), it is important that we build fundamental knowledge and resilience about risk in research so that we can put in place mechanisms to deal with the risks that may arise, especially after gaining ethical approval. Drawing from our practical experiences in conducting research across diverse cohorts as well as key literature, we identify several critical risk areas that guide our approach to qualitative criminological research. The following points provide a foundational framework, necessitating further elaboration contingent upon the specific risk factors inherent in each research project.

Risk in Sensitive Research

The likelihood of undertaking research of a sensitive criminological nature is prevalent, particularly in the context of discourses focussing on criminal behaviour, victimisation, and trauma. Risks inherent in sensitive research have been raised by a range of scholars who have carried out pioneering qualitative studies (Hobbs, 1995; Hallsworth, 2013; Salinas, 2017; Bakkali, 2019). Very few, however, have offered practical advice on how to deal with issues that may arise upon ethical approval. We believe that one of the most obvious, effective, yet overlooked forms of aftercare is to hold a debrief session. This is also recommended by Healy (2009), who notes that holding a debrief session offers an opportunity for participants to 'wind down' after the interview and to ask questions about the research. We argue that in addition to the information offered on a debrief sheet, holding a meeting also presents the opportunity to design a bespoke protocol or an intervention to deal with any distress that may occur. From our collective experiences, debrief meetings have aided our research outcomes, as they serve as a conduit to learn further through discussion and reflection of events.

Holding a debrief meeting is a highly beneficial practical exercise to clarify any misconceptions, improve recall, and formulate any rectifications during data collection. It also aids the rapport between the researcher and participant. However, to maintain an ethical relationship between the researcher and participant, it is highly advisable that any debrief meeting has structure. For an effective debrief, we encourage researchers to plan the meeting in advance, ensure that it takes place in a safe space, review the meeting aims, take notes, be transparent, and conclude with a brief recap and an understanding of what will take place in the future.

Physical Risks

Criminological research that consists of certain qualitative methods and topics may result in a range of physical risks and ethical upheavals. For example, ethnographic research on marginalised communities, crimes of the poor, vulnerable people, criminal syndicates, prisoners and more, can conjure possible physical risks. From our collective experiences, ethnographic research can put ethics committees at discomfort as this form of scientific study conventionally requires the immersion of the researcher(s) in spaces and places occupied by those that are researched, which by design reduces the social distance between the researcher(s) and the researched (Yates, 2004). Commentators have also expressed how ethnography can expose researchers to illegal practice (Salinas, 2017), fear (Hobbs & May, 1993), as well as the potential to cause harm to respondents (Ryder, 2021).

Despite the above criticisms, ethnography remains one of the most notable, purest, and richest qualitative research methods in criminological scholarship, yielding pioneering contributions on a global scale. While it is often criticised for lacking research generalisability, it indisputably excels in providing rich datasets for participants that are often voiceless and frequently marginalised in mainstream society. While Chapter 3 offers detailed insights on how Deuchar navigated risks as an ethnographer, all while producing cutting-edge research, the following are some practical tips that have helped us manage physical risks.

GET TO KNOW RESEARCH IN YOUR FIELD

Since ethnography is an established qualitative method in social sciences, there is ample generic literature on the method itself as well as subject-specific texts. Generic reading will allow researchers to appreciate the core tenets of the method, whereas subject-specific will help the acquisition of in-depth knowledge on the area, expert perspectives, research skills, critical thinking skills, and professional development. Above all, reading will serve as a guide to understand the successes of a project, the pitfalls, and where future work requires development.

ADOPT AN ETHICAL POSITION

Ensure that your work has a robust ethical framework that can guide you to conduct research as well as safeguard you from issues that could arise. A good starting point is to adhere to the code of human research ethics of the researcher's university. For academics and those affiliated with an organisation or someone who is working independently, additional guidance is available from professional bodies online, such as the British Society of Criminology, British Sociological Association, British Psychological Society, National Youth Agency, and UK Research and Innovation.

LOOK WITHIN AND IDENTIFY YOUR STRENGTHS

We often encourage our peers to look within before conducting fieldwork. By this, we urge researchers to focus on the *capitals* at their disposal when undertaking research. In their work on interdisciplinary scholarship, Thompson et al. (2016) noted the overlapping set of resources that can foster research activity. They considered: *human capital*, described as technical skills and knowledge, or 'what you know'; *cultural capital*, an enculturated set of norms, values, and dispositions, or 'how you know'; and *social capital*, interpersonal connections that provide access to resources and information, or 'who you know'.

An application of this, for example, is Rahman et al.'s (2020) research on criminal enforcement that examined pathways into extra-legal governance within the UK underworld. The findings were based on several semi-structured interviews with men that were part of organised crime networks in the West of Scotland and the West Midlands. The research team for the study comprising four scholars: Mohammed Rahman (the lead researcher who carried out fieldwork in the West Midlands), Robert McLean (co-author who carried out fieldwork in the West of Scotland), Ross Deuchar (co-author with global expertise on criminal networks), and James Densley (co-author with global expertise on criminal networks). All of the researchers were knowledgeable in conducting qualitative research with people from offending backgrounds. This served as one of their main forms of human capital. The scholars knew each other in a professional capacity for several years before undertaking the research. They had a strong understanding of each other's academic credentials, discipline experiences, and publishing history, which helped the acquisition of cultural capital. In terms of social capital, Rahman and McLean were able to gain access to criminal enforcers based on previous research. As they had a pre-existing rapport with their participants, this considerably minimised physical risks towards them and their participants.

The illustration above shows that researchers can significantly lessen physical risks in their work by effectively using their capitals as resources. We understand, however, that some researchers may not have the ability to do team-based research or have enough experience to access existing networks. Hence, the next two points can help researchers from any background or level of experience.

GO BEYOND ONE RESEARCH METHOD

Researchers are often fixed on one research method to acquire data. However, we encourage the use of either mixed or multiple methods so as to be able to triangulate, develop and expand research. For instance, Deuchar's (2018) multi-site study offered an eclectic understanding of religiosity and spirituality in the context of gang membership desistance. Alongside his primary methodology of ethnography, Deuchar used a cocktail of methodologies that included data collection via life histories, semi-structured interviews, and observations. Similarly, Rahman's (2019) study on serious violence and organised crime in the West Midlands generated qualitative data from ethnography, ethnographic content analysis, semi-structured interviews, and case studies. Certain aspects of Rahman's research also required the analysis of court data to verify primary accounts. Taking a multiple method approach for Deuchar and Rahman allowed them to primarily offer rich and reliable datasets, widen the scope and breadth of their studies, and provide greater insights and perspectives.

Important here is to acknowledge the significance of secondary datasets in qualitative research. Research on the extent of violent practice in the motorcycle underworld by Rahman and Lynes (2018, p. 7) was conducted through the triangulation of a case study and a biographical account in order to theorise murder within outlaw motorcycle clubs. The authors justified their secondary datasets by stating that case study research offers scholars a variety of ways to examine new research areas in some depth. They also noted that biographical data offers an 'in-depth account of criminal careers, of which most academic work overlooks or fails to achieve'. This example illustrates that research on sensitive topics can be carried out through a secondary qualitative approach all while preventing any physical risk.

SEEK WISDOM FROM THOSE THAT ARE MORE EXPERIENCED

New and early career researchers can benefit from being mentored by experienced researchers. A research mentor should be able to provide helpful advice and insights into various facets of carrying out academic research. Undergraduate and postgraduate students are often assigned to a research supervisor, ideally with aligned expertise to the research subject. The supervisor has the responsibility to provide regular guidance through effective communication. From our experiences of supervising undergraduate, postgraduate, and PhD dissertations, we have been able to assess any risks associated with student projects and how best to tackle them.

For those who want to undertake research but are not affiliated with an academic institution, there are several ways that a research mentor can be found. Most academics who are researchers will have an online presence. Finding an academic that has similar interests is crucial. Do not limit yourself to one subject specialist, especially if you have multidisciplinary interests. If you have also previously studied, think about past experiences that you have enjoyed and consider the academic who taught you to be your mentor. Most researchers are extremely approachable, and we would encourage exploring the work of whom you wish to be mentored by before contacting them.

Emotional Risks

While Chapter 4 is dedicated to the emotional labour of carrying out criminological research and its management, it is briefly worthwhile noting here that the likelihood of researchers undertaking sensitive research and being exposed to emotional risk is relatively high (Widdowfield, 2000; Nielsen, 2010; Garrihy & Watters, 2020). Research that involves the coverage of criminality and victimisation, coupled with face-to-face qualitative inquiries can have an emotional cost for researchers. Rahman (2019, p. 143) drew attention to the default emotional labour associated with ethnomethodological studies and noted the importance of researchers treating research subjects with integrity, compassion, and empathy.

> Integrity is a crucial characteristic that should be central to all aspects of academic inquiry. Often, however, compassion is confused with empathy. Compassion is widely defined as the ability to understand the emotional state of an individual. Having compassion entails the desire to alleviate suffering. So too, empathy, as most people know of it, is the ability to literally or figuratively put yourself in the position of another person. If ethnographers incorporate these traits in their work, naturally it will generate novel studies that exude academic rigour.

To take a compassionate approach by the researcher to those that they research is an ethical virtue, yet one that can be emotionally intensive. This makes emotions in research a double-edged sword. As Burkitt (2012, p. 459) reminds us:

> Emotion is not just something that we reflect on in a disengaged way, it is central to the way people in social relations relate to one another: it is woven into the fabric of the interactions we are engaged in and it is therefore also central to the way we relate to ourselves as well as to others.

Bergman and Wettergren (2015) consider the emotional labour associated with qualitative research as an integral part of the job. Irrespective of this being the case, researchers should foresee any potential emotional risk that they or their participants may be exposed to and should put in place mechanisms that can proficiently navigate and manage the emotional dimensions inherent in the research process.

Research training is often delivered through modules on formal courses. However, very little attention has been given in criminological discourse to what type of training and supervision researchers need to carry out for engaging in sensitive research. In their study on managing risks and ethics in research, Dickson-Swift et al. (2008) highlighted how their participants in the health sector emphasised a focus on the skills needed to talk with people that are exposed to vulnerability, with some of their respondents highlighting the desire to undergo counseling training. However, in criminological research, participants are often signposted by researchers to organisations that offer professional support to mitigate any physical and psychological risks.

We believe that participant safeguarding is paramount when working with vulnerable cohorts and sensitive topics. Therefore, it is important for researchers to identify appropriate organisations that can support participants. Organisations should be identified based on subject-matter specialisms. In our studies, we have habitually signposted our participants to 24-hour helplines, mental health charities, and/or victim support groups. In addition, during our fieldwork, we periodically check in with participants in instances where we believe that the consequences of partaking in our research may have ramifications to cause an adverse impact. We encourage others to do the same as this helps assess whether initial signposting remains appropriate for participants or whether additional support is required.

RISK ASSESSMENT

Like many Western nations, in the UK, all employees are covered by the Health and Safety at Work etc Act 1974. Under this legislation, it sets out the general duties which:

a.   employers have towards employees and members of the public;
b.   employees have to themselves and to each other;
c.   certain self-employed have towards themselves and others.

Lee-Treweek and Linkogle (2000, p. 197) note that researchers should be aware that as employees of institutions 'the risks they face can be considered within the framework of employment legislation designed to protect all workers'. Equally, institutions that are research focussed have an obligation to ensure that potential harm to researchers is minimised. For further information on risk assessment and safeguarding, researchers should seek advice from an ethics committee or Human Resources.

Conclusion

This chapter explored key issues that researchers need to address before commencing research. We discussed how research projects undergo thorough screening to gauge inherent risks, such as the involvement of human participation, data confidentiality, and the exploration of sensitive topics. Any project deemed to be of high risk will go through additional scrutiny by specialised committees. The notion of safeguarding in research covers several dimensions, of which include: the age and vulnerability of participants and the potential for breaches of confidentiality. Basic project information, justification, and potential benefits are crucial aspects of an ethics application, with a focus on a clear and realistic project timeframe. We argue that any research project application submitted for ethical approval should contextualise the project with existing academic literature. Not only is this academically sound, but it will also aid reviewers to understand the project's wider contribution.

We highlighted through an example that researchers may face challenges in participant recruitment, especially for sensitive criminological topics. By having a predefined criterion, Rahman and Abdulkader (2022) alleviated this issue as their study on the vulnerabilities associated with rough sleepers took a purposive sampling approach. While this had some limitations, they managed to prevent any data manipulation through extensive reflexivity and collaboration with caseworkers. Their engagement with caseworkers and the meticulous consideration of suitable participants exemplifies a thoroughly planned and ethical research process. The example also presented the importance of reflexivity as a safeguard against potential criticism, and the involvement of caseworkers enhances the ability to minimise risks associated with vulnerable populations. This chapter offered excerpts submitted by Rahman and Abdulkader for ethical approval, which emphasise the necessity of justifying data collection methods in an ethics application. Their use of a focus group was supported by existing literature and practical viability.

The relevance of maintaining research anonymity and confidentiality was explored in this chapter. In cases where both cannot be guaranteed, robust justifications must be offered to the ethics committee. Data storage, data transfer, and data destruction processes are crucial to upholding ethical principles. Researchers have a default obligation to comply with GDPR and the UK Data Protection Act. We stressed in this chapter the importance of researchers remaining vigilant about potential changes in their project post-ethical approval. Modifications such as adopting a new research method or altering an existing one may occur, ergo impacting participant engagement, data collection approaches and fieldwork locations. The example of Rahman's (2019) ethnographic inquiry on organised crime in the West Midlands, England, revealed how advancements in technology can revolutionise conventional data collection. While researchers may find efficient ways to collect data during fieldwork, any changes necessitate the revisiting of an approved application so that justification is offered for new approaches as well as the consideration of research feasibility. This underscores the dynamic nature of criminological research and the significance of transparent and ethical adaptations throughout a study. A research project may also require modification due to unforeseen circumstances. We exemplified this through the illustration of Rahman and Abdulkader (2022), who moved in person interviews to online during the COVID-19 pandemic. The chapter drew attention to how the change was not a mere transition. Rather, the researchers extensively assessed appropriateness when obtaining informed consent online, upholding confidentiality and managing digital data.

The practice of methodological reflexivity was discussed through existing literature and its role in making nuanced ethical decisions amid evolving research contexts. While we advocate the practice of reflexivity and its benefits of mitigating potential risks, it is important to acknowledge that complete risk elimination is not guaranteed in research. Therefore, we present an understanding of multiple risks for both researchers and participants, particularly in the engagement of sensitive criminological research. Through literature and our own research experiences, our discussion stresses the need for researchers to acknowledge and navigate potential risks after gaining ethical approval. Practical advice that we offer in this chapter includes holding debrief sessions for sensitive research, managing physical risks through knowledge, ethical positioning, and diversified research methods. Furthermore, emotional risks, often linked with face-to-face inquiries, are highlighted, emphasising the significance of integrity, compassion, and empathy. We also drew attention to the need for additional support mechanisms, such as participant safeguarding and risk assessments under existing employment legislation, to ensure the well-being of both researchers and participants.

References

Armstrong, G. (1993) Like that Desmond Morris?. In D. Hobbs & T. May (eds.), *Interpreting the field: Accounts of ethnography*. Oxford: Oxford University Press, 3–43.

Bakkali, Y. (2019) Dying to live: Youth violence and munpain. *The Sociological Review*, 67(6), 1317–1332.

Beck, U. (1992) *Risk society*. London: Sage.

Bergman Blix, S., & Wettergren, Å. (2015)The emotional labour of gaining and maintaining access to the field.*Qualitative Research*, 15(6), 688–704.

British Society of Criminology (2015) Statement of ethics. Available at: <https://www.britsoccrim.org/documents/BSCEthics2015.pdf>. Last accessed: 28 February 2024.

Bryman, A. (2016) *Social research methods*. Oxford: Oxford University Press.

Burkitt, I. (2012) Emotional reflexivity: Feeling, emotion and imagination in reflexive dialogues. *Sociology*, 46(3), 458–472.

Burnard, P. (2011) A pragmatic approach to qualitative data analysis. In R. Newell & P. Burnard (eds.), *Research for evidence-based practice in healthcare*. London: Wiley–Blackwell, 118–129.

Cheng, C., & Kumar, V. (2012) Pattern of exploitation and organised crime: Study on homeless beggars in Patna, Bihar. *International Journal of Scientific and Research Publications*, 2(11), 1–5.

Deuchar, R. (2018) *Gangs & spirituality: Global perspectives*. Switzerland: Palgrave MacMillan.

Dickson-Swift, V., James, E. L., & Liamputtong, P. (2008) *Undertaking sensitive research in the health and social sciences: Managing boundaries, emotions and risks*. Cambridge: Cambridge University Press.

Emmel, N. (2013)*Sampling and choosing cases in qualitative research: A realist approach*. London: Sage.

Finlay, L. (2002) Negotiating the swamp: The opportunity and challenge of reflexivity in research practice. *Qualitative Research*, 2(2), 209–230.

Fox, N. (1998) Risks, hazards and life choices: Reflections on health at work. *Sociology*, 32(4), 665–687.

Fujimura, C. (2003) Adult stigmatization and the hidden power of homeless children in Russia. *Children, Youth, and Environments*, 13(1), 1546–2250.

Garrihy, J., & Watters, A. (2020) Emotions and agency in prison research. *Methodological Innovations*, 13(2), 1–14.

Giddens, A. (1991) *Modernity and self-identity: Self and society in the late modern age*. Cambridge: Polity Press.

Gunter, A. (2010) *Growing up bad? Black youth 'road' culture and badness in an East London neighborhood*. London: Tufnell Press.

Hallsworth, S. (2013) *The gang and beyond: Interpreting violent street worlds*. London: Palgrave.

Hammersley, M. (1992) Deconstructing the qualitative-quantitative divide. In J. Brannen (ed.), *Mixing methods: Qualitative and quantitative research*. Aldershot: Avebury, 39–55.

Harper, L., Kalfa, N., Beckers, G. M. A., Kaefer, M., Nieuwhof-Leppink, A. J., Fossum, M., Herbst, K. W., & Bagli, D. (2020) The impact of COVID-19 on research. *Journal of Pediatric Urology*, 16(5), 715–716.

Healy, D. (2009) Ethics and criminological research: Charting a way forward. *Irish Probation Journal*, 6 (1), 171–182.

Hobbs, D. (1995) *Bad business: Professional criminals in modern britain*. Oxford: Oxford University Press.

Hobbs, D., & May, T. (1993) *Interpreting the field: Accounts of ethnography*. Oxford: Oxford University Press.

Lee-Treweek, G., & Linkogle, S. (2000) *Danger in the field: Risk and ethics in social research*. London: Routledge.

Lichterman, P. (2016) Interpretive reflexivity in ethnography. *Ethnography*, 18(1), 35–45.

Lupton, D. (2002) Risk is part of your life: Risk epistemologies among a group of Australians. *Sociology*, 36(2), 317–334.

Marcus, G. E. (2021) *Ethnography through thick and thin.* Princeton, NJ: Princeton University Press.

Nielsen, M. M. (2010) Pains and possibilities in prison: On the use of emotions and positioning in ethnographic research. *Acta Sociologica,* 53(4), 307–321.

Olmos-Vega, F. M., Stalmeijer, R. E., Varpio, L., & Kahlke, R. (2022) A practical guide to reflexivity in qualitative research: AMEE guide No. 149. *Medical Teacher,* 45(3), 241–251.

Polit, D., & Beck, C. (2009) *Essentials of nursing research: Appraising evidence for nursing practice.* PA: Wolters Kluwer Health/Lippincott Williams & Wilkins.

Rahman, M. (2016) Understanding organised crime and fatal violence in Birmingham: A case study of the 2003 new year shootings. Papers from the British Criminology Conference, Vol 16.

Rahman, M (2019) *Homicide and organised crime: Ethnographic narratives of serious violence within the criminal underworld.* London: Palgrave.

Rahman, M., & Abdulkader, M. (2022) Living rough: An exploratory study on the vulnerabilities of rough sleepers in Birmingham, United Kingdom. *Abuse: An International Impact Journal,* 3(1), 22–42.

Rahman, M., & Lynes, A. (2018) Ride to die: Understanding masculine honour and collective identity in the motorcycle underworld. *Journal of Criminological Research, Policy and Practice,* 4(4), 238–252.

Rahman, M., McLean, R., Deuchar, R., & Densley, J. (2020) Who are the enforcers? The motives and methods of muscle for hire in West Scotland and the West Midlands. *Trends in Organized Crime,* 25(1), 108–129.

Ryder, A. (2021) Critical ethnography and research relationships: Some ethical dilemmas. *Anthropology and Humanism,* 46(2), 300–314.

Salinas, M. (2017) The unusual suspects: An educated, legitimately employed drug dealing network. *International Criminal Justice Review,* 28(3), 226–242.

Scheurich, J. (1997) *Research method in the postmodern.* London: Routledge.

Stoecker, A. W. (2001) Homelessness and criminal exploitation of Russian minors: Realities, resources, and legal remedies. *Demokratizatsiya; Washington,* 9(2), 319–336.

Thompson J. J., Conaway E., & Dolan E. L. (2016) Undergraduate students' development of social, cultural, and human capital in a networked research experience. *Cultural Studies of Science Education,* 11(4), 959–990.

UK Research and Innovation (2021) Survey findings of the impact of COVID-19 on researchers. Available at: <https://www.ukri.org/news/survey-findings-of-the -impact-of-covid-19-on-researchers/>. Last accessed 28 February 2024.

Varpio, L., Paradis, E., Uijtdehaage, S., & Young, M. (2020) The distinctions between theory, theoretical framework, and conceptual framework. *Acad Med,* 95(7), 989–994.

Walsh, R. (2003) The methods of reflexivity. *Humanist Psychol,* 31(4), 51–66.

Widdowfield, R. (2000) The place of emotions in academic research. *Area,* 32(2), 199–208.

Yates, J. (2004) Criminological ethnography: Risks, dilemmas and their negotiation. *British Journal of Community Justice,* 3(1), 19–32.

Zhang, R., Brennan, T. J., & Lo, A. W. (2014) The origin of risk aversion. *PNAS,* 111(50), 17777–17782.

3 Dealing with Boundaries

Negotiating Boundaries, Disclosure, and Ethical Covertness

Introduction

Qualitative Research, Impression Management, and Boundaries

As criminologists, we tend to rely on empirical research with human participants, the majority of whom are lawbreakers, ranging from petty delinquents right through to perpetrators of the most heinous crimes (Johnstone, 2005). At other times, we may draw upon the experiences of those who have been affected by, or whose job it is to reduce or prevent, criminal acts – with the latter including police officers, prison officers, youth, community and social workers or members of the judiciary (ibid). For qualitative researchers, the process of data gathering in the field also involves actively observing, listening to, or even participating with, members of our empirical samples and interpreting their 'self-understandings' and lived experiences (Grant & Giddings, 2002, p. 16). If we take a radical approach to our data collection and analysis, we may seek to emancipate the most disadvantaged and vulnerable from unjust and oppressive social structures by seeking to use our research to empower them to engage in 'collective action and struggle' (Grant & Giddings, 2002, p. 19). The latter may be particularly relevant to criminologists working with participants who have been disempowered by agents of social control and via their experiences in the criminal justice system. These approaches all suggest the need for us, as researchers, to hold onto and actively promote key values such as reciprocity, empathy and power-sharing while also maintaining appropriate professional boundaries and a level of social distance. This creates the need for a careful balancing act, and at times can lead to a blurring of boundaries that become central to the research process.

In qualitative approaches to criminology, the use of the interview is a particularly relevant means of collecting data on sensitive subjects. It is seen as a very appropriate means of exploring personal experiences, social contexts, and motivations. Jensen (2012) argues that conducting interviews involves a process of identity formation whereby the researcher invites his/her participants to speak from specific subject positions. In criminology, this often involves researchers actively calling participants to step back into their previous (or,

DOI: 10.4324/9781003304746-3

in some cases, current) offender roles and identities to describe their lived experiences, motivations, and perspectives. In all of this, the researcher needs to ensure that an appropriate level of rapport is established, trust is built, and empathy is displayed to enhance the richness of the data (Deuchar, 2015).

However, while building rapport and demonstrating empathy and compassion for participants is an essential means of researchers encouraging participants to open up emotionally and ultimately to facilitate deeper and richer data, to what lengths should this be taken? How do researchers know how best to place boundaries around this process? As Gemignani (2011, p. 701) argues, distancing oneself from the emotive issues that participants may want to open up about may enable the researcher to feel 'safer'. However, it may also lead to participants feeling excluded or abandoned, thus in turn reinforcing the 'emotional isolation and incommunicability' that many offenders have experienced due to issues relating to trauma.

In cases where the researcher uses qualitative interviews that lend themselves to participants sharing sensitive and controversial personal insights, impression management may become important (Goffman, 1959; Hammersley & Atkinson, 1983; Drake & Harvey, 2014; Deuchar, 2015). Goffman (1961, p. 7) argued that 'any group of persons – prisoners, primitives, pilots or patients – develop a life of their own that becomes meaningful, reasonable, and normal once you get close to it'. Accordingly, he contended that a good way to learn about these worlds is to 'submit oneself to the company of the members to the daily round of petty contingencies to which they are subject' (ibid). This is particularly relevant where such interviews are conducted within the wider context of an ethnographic study involving the researcher spending a significant period participating alongside those with a history of criminality. In doing so, Goffman argued that ethnographic researchers engage in 'front-stage' and 'back-stage' performances whereby the way they present themselves to participants will often be quite different from their normal behaviour.

Building on this, Drake and Harvey (2014, p. 493) suggest that the ethnographer needs to manage his/her role in these varying contexts through a range of 'virtual identities', essentially adopting a 'chameleon-like identity'. This impression management 'performance' can ultimately serve to blur the traditional boundaries between the researcher and researched, while at the same time placing a considerable strain on the researcher, particularly if, for example, research participants hold views that are diametrically opposed to those of the academic (Drake & Harvey, 2014). For instance, some criminologists report finding it hard to identify with their subjects due to their offending and (in some cases) violent lifestyles and view themselves as complete 'outsiders' (for discussion, see Worley et al., 2016). On the other hand, we cannot ignore the potential for ethnographers to 'go native' and to assume the cultural traits of their participants, while also literally taking on their pain (Gemignani, 2011). In such cases, researchers may become so immersed in the research that reactivity reduces, and they literally transform into 'fully-fledged members of the subculture' and become 'insiders' (Worley et al., 2016, p. 299). Beyens et al. (2015, p. 71) refer to the careful balancing act of being 'sufficiently involved [with] and being appropriately detached from ... research subjects', while also drawing attention to the risks inherent in allowing the research subject's 'views, rhetoric or behaviour' to uncritically take over. The above discussion leads us to reflect on some important dilemmas. How can we as qualitative criminological researchers achieve the right balance between seeing ourselves as 'insiders' or 'outsiders'? Further, how can we recognise if and when we are getting too involved or allowing our relationship with participants to negatively impact upon our capacity for criticality?

Negotiating Boundaries and Ethics of Care

As we have alluded to, spending significant time in the field and within social contexts that are intimately familiar to those involved in committing, or perhaps even those who are seeking to prevent, criminality, ultimately involves the building of trusting relationships. These relationships can, however, be influenced by a range of factors including age, appearance, social class, gender, and environment (Hewitt, 2007). Hewitt (2007, p. 1150) highlights that the quality of the relationship may often depend on 'perceptions of professional boundaries' and the related capacity for intimacy and informality.

Some academic literature (Bourne, 1998; Richards & Emslie, 2000; Hewitt, 2007) asserts that there is a similarity between research interviews, participant observation, and therapeutic psychological encounters. Accordingly, 'person-centred skills' required to develop research relationships and maintain engagement may often be similar to those required within a therapist–patient context (Hewitt, 2007, p. 1153). Adopting a therapeutic approach to qualitative interviewing and observation may not only elicit deeper levels of data but also have a cathartic effect on the research participant. However, there is also the risk that, as criminologists, the process of probing for deeper levels of insight into participants' personal beliefs and behaviour may also lead to anxiety, distress, guilt, and damage to participants' self-esteem if this becomes too intrusive (ibid, and see also Hammersley & Atkinson, 2007). Thus, a balance often needs to be sought between the need for building empathetic, trusting relationships that enable research participants to open up about their experiences and the need for adopting an 'ethics-of-care perspective' – in short, as criminological researchers, how do we balance the need for 'rigour' with the need for 'moral concerns'? (ibid, p. 1156).

Added to this, while spending extended time in the field with participants, ethnographers will inevitably need to share aspects of their own personal histories, lived experiences, interests, values and structural positioning. Earlier we touched on the balance between engaging in impression management and the risks involved in 'going native'. Sharpe (2017) draws attention to the dichotomy of the 'insider/outsider' research perspective. While presenting oneself as an 'outsider' in relation to social class, positioning and/or life experience may elicit greater disclosure by participants, it may also (particularly when working with ex- or current offenders) impede rapport and potentially cause suspicion on the part of participants regarding the researcher's motives (ibid).

Inevitably, it is true to say that a certain degree of power imbalance will always exist between the researcher and researched, in spite of attempts made by the former to establish egalitarian, reciprocal relationships (Hewitt, 2007). Interestingly, some scholarship has suggested that a certain degree of antagonistic interaction can lead to valuable data. For instance, as a White male researcher working in Denmark, Jensen (2012, p. 128) described his experiences of working with young black men who tended to react to him as if he was a 'symbol of white ethnic Danish society which they felt excluded from'. He found that they did not 'passively subjugate themselves to the authority of white middle-class masculinity' but rather reacted with resistance or reluctance. Jensen highlights that the antagonistic nature of some of these interactions added an important dimension to the research findings, given that it illustrated that these young men tended to resist and disidentify from the position of the 'problematic other' (ibid).

At the most extreme end of the 'insider/outsider' continuum lies the use of covert ethnography. Although generally now frowned upon in the current climate of 'increased regimentation and regulation', Calvey (2013, p. 542) highlights that it has a clear place in the history of criminological ethnography and should still be a part of the 'standard methodological toolkit'. He goes on to argue that the tendency for covert research to be treated as an 'antithesis to open and overt research' represents a very simplistic duality, since there is not a clear and polarised divide between overt and covert research (ibid). Further, Van Deventer (2009, p. 51) highlights that, even where ethnographers are upfront about their research intentions to those around them, 'a certain amount of covertness' will always be involved in their fieldwork. In short, the study of crime may sometimes invite or even require subtle forms of deception and covert methods that compel ethnographers to deviate from idealised ethical guidelines (Fine, 1993; Miller, 1995; Calvey, 2013; Deuchar, 2015).

All of this leads us to some important questions – how much should the researcher disclose about his/her own life, perspectives, and values and how much should be withheld? To what extent should the researcher strive to avoid antagonism, and is it always harmful to allow this to occur? And is there a place for covertness, particularly in ethnographic criminology, and how can researchers engage in this while still upholding ethical and moral standards?

The questions and dilemmas we have raised in the early part of this chapter are ones that we as authors have grappled with for many years. The remainder of the chapter draws upon illustrative examples from Deuchar's own research to enable him to provide some reflexive accounts of how he has navigated boundaries and identified strategies to find some middle ground while working at the sharp end of criminological fieldwork. In the sections that follow, we therefore offer some potential suggestions that may be helpful for other researchers to contemplate during their own methodological journeys.

Tales from the Field: Illustrative Examples and Reflexive Accounts: The Balance between Being an 'Insider' or 'Outsider'

During the course of his international ethnographic research on street gangs, gang intervention, and desistance, Deuchar had the opportunity to travel to Los Angeles, USA, on more than one occasion to conduct fieldwork. He spent several weeks participating in and observing therapeutic interventions within *Homeboy Industries* [the largest gang intervention and rehabilitation programme in the country]. The support programmes there draw upon eclectic forms of spirituality which, rather than focussing on religion, place an emphasis on nurturing transcendent experiences in a spiritual, but largely secular, way (for further discussion, see Deuchar, 2018). The following extract from Deuchar's (2018) fieldnotes illustrates his experience of participating alongside reforming gang members, the majority of whom were Latino (and, more specifically, of Mexican descent), as they engaged in group therapy sessions. Following the extract, and writing in the first person, Deuchar uses this as an illustrative example of how ethnographers like ourselves often have to balance a focus on attachment and detachment during the course of our fieldwork.

Illustrative Example 1: Participant Observation in 'Homeboy Industries'

Early on Thursday morning I participate in the 'Healing Circle', which today is being led by a middle-aged white woman named Anna. There are 12 of us in the room sitting on the floor. Anna lights up a candle and what looks like some incense in a half shell in front of her. As she passes the shell and a short wooden stick around the room I begin to become aware of the strong aroma emanating from it. Anna explains that the shell contains a particular type of Californian herb with healing qualities. 'Ok so as I pass round the shell and the talking stick, each of you just say a little bit about your highs and lows.'

As the stick and the incense moves around the room, each person says something slightly different. 'Hi, my name is Fernando and I'm pretty good today,' one Latino young man says. 'Hi, my name is Mick and I'm generally good,' another young black man adds. 'My name is Martha and there's still some shit going on but I'm getting there,' one of the Latino young women responds. 'Hi, I'm Jack and I've just got visiting rights to my son which is good. He's still a little shy with me but at least he's getting to know me,' adds a slightly older Latino man who looks as if he is in his early thirties. 'Hi, last week I found out that I lost my rights to see my kids. I'm beginning to get there now, but I just wanna thank Miguel and Heidi for all their support because I know I was a mess last Friday and I wouldn't have got through it without them.' As this young Latino woman makes this statement, I notice that Miguel and Heidi are sitting on the floor beside her and smile and nod kindly.

Now the incense is passed to me. 'Hi, I'm Ross and I'm from Scotland ... I'm a criminologist in a university there. I've had a wonderful time here and it's just been a privilege to meet you all and hear about your challenges and some of the wonderful stories of transformation. I've learned a lot from you on this, the way you share and give to each other – that makes a tremendous difference.' Anna then takes the stick and the incense and continues, 'you know what Ross said is so important – it's that sharing, that talking and healing that is so important. We can talk openly here – we can cry if we want.'

The next day I participate in the 'Street Poetry' class. Each of the 'home-boys' and 'homegirls' share poems and narratives they have written, expressing their personal emotions, struggles and feelings. Two men from Street Poets are facilitating. Street Poets is a non-profit poetry-based peace-making organisation dedicated to the creative process as a force for individual and community transformation (see Deuchar, 2018). The poets talk to the participants about choices – the harder choice, they explain, is to be here in this class sharing insights and engaging in personal develop-ment: 'You're all trying to re-educate yourselves, and that's harder than being on the block.'

The facilitators ask if anyone else feels ready to share their work. One young Latino man in his late twenties, whose name is Jesus, reads out a thought-provoking poem about his deepest emotions and challenges. The description is amazing, and it is clear that this young man has a talent for writing. One of the street poets snaps his fingers in approval. 'You know you got a beautiful mind, man – now you have this gift, you need to look for the cracks of light to come in because once we write things down, the process begins ... as street poets, we have this identity as wounded heal-ers – not getting away from the wounds but getting closer to them. You know, brother, we live in a city with millions of people in it – but every one of us is lonely ... but by sharing that piece, you are beginning to create a community ... you were in prison for 18 years, but now you're back, man, and you should share your gifts ... these gifts can be like medicine to a sick culture. It's like you have been in prison – you have experienced the poison ... but in doing so you have something with which to heal others.'

At this point, we all stand up and we bow our heads to say the serenity prayer. Once again, I feel the strong feeling of kinship in the room that I have felt many times over the course of my visit. As I leave the room, I am fascinated by the continual focus on personal and mutual affirmation that emerges from these therapy sessions.

(Researcher's fieldnotes, reproduced from Deuchar, 2018)

'INSIDER/OUTSIDER' REFLECTIONS BY DEUCHAR

In the above example, I fluctuated between participation and observation during both therapy sessions. In the first session, my role was one of participant-as-observer (Gold, 1958) where I presented myself largely as an active participant in the healing circle. I sat on the floor beside the reforming gang members (commonly referred to as 'trainees' during their participation in *Homeboy Industries*). I actively listened to their emotional insights while also accepting the offer of the incense stick and sharing my own thoughts alongside them. The young men and women who were present had suffered from considerable trauma, leading to addiction and – ultimately – gang-related violence and criminality (see Deuchar, 2018). This became most apparent to me when the incense was passed to the young Latino mother, who opened up emotionally about losing the rights to keep her children (apparently as a result of her addiction and her gang-involved lifestyle).

All of the staff and trainees in *Homeboy Industries* had been informed about my research intentions when I first arrived there, through announcements that were made by senior management during early morning collective icebreaker sessions and via information sheets that I had distributed. As such, they had been made aware of my presence and the fact that I may be observing them during rehabilitation sessions. However, prior consent to be observed had mostly been gathered via an 'opt out' system, where participants were asked to make me aware if they were unwilling to be observed. It may have been the case that some participants had not been present during the icebreakers or had overlooked the distributed information, and during the 'healing circle' I initially made no attempt to refer back to the nature and purpose of my research. My involvement was principally one of participant, where I was also observing. By adopting this role, I was effectively adopting the role of 'insider'- blending in with the trainees and the therapist and therefore putting those around me at ease, since I felt it would be inappropriate to divert the conversation onto my research when participants were clearly opening up emotionally about sensitive issues.

In becoming a practical 'insider', or 'marginal native' (Deuchar, 2015), to some extent I was introducing a certain degree of covertness to the fieldwork process. This subtle form of deception caused me some angst, and at a certain point I recognised the need to step back into the research role more fully and remind those around me of my role and the reason for my presence (Fine, 1993; Miller, 1995; Calvey, 2013; Deuchar, 2015). Accordingly, when the turn came to take the incense and contribute to the group, I used the opportunity to refer to my professional role while also engaging in a certain amount of impression management to provide positive affirmations to the group and to share what I had learned (Goffman, 1959; Hammersley & Atkinson, 2007; Drake & Harvey, 2014; Deuchar, 2015).

Drake & Harvey (2014, p. 494) argue that the primary goal of the ethnographer is to become 'attuned to the context(s) of the environment and culture(s) they are studying'. To become sufficiently attuned, they argue that he/she must 'strive towards a sense of mastery' despite the fact that the 'known observer can never really belong' (ibid). In striving towards fully understanding the backdrop and context that characterised the reforming gang members' lives in Los Angeles, including the addiction and trauma they had suffered, the consequences of this and the place of lived experience and group therapy in supporting their transformation journeys, at times I found myself adopting a 'chameleon-like identity' (Drake & Harvey, 2014, p. 493). I thus fluctuated between attachment and detachment during my fieldwork. As the above extract illustrates, I moved from being attached during the 'healing circle' to becoming detached the next day during the 'street poetry' session where I was initially simply observing the men as they shared their writing, before then moving back from 'outsider' to partial 'insider' to engage with the participants in the sharing of the serenity prayer at the end of the session.

However, although I often felt like a partial 'insider', I was also constantly aware – as a White male from Scotland – that my ability to have a full appreciation of the subordination and marginalisation of people of colour in the American context, how this had been created, maintained and its impact on my black and Latino participants, would always have its limitations (Villenas & Deyhle, 1999; Deuchar et al., 2021). Therefore, my role as an 'outsider' invariably became the dominant one.

Disclosure and Avoiding Antagonism

During his early work on street gang culture and youth violence in Glasgow, Scotland (see Deuchar, 2009), Deuchar quickly became aware of the need to establish the trust of his young participants through impression management (Fine, 1993). On visits to youth clubs and subsequent meetings in secure accommodation and prisons, he thus ensured that he dressed in a particular way (usually in t-shirts, hooded tops, and jeans) and also adapted the way he spoke, deliberately adopting a more informal language while actively using humour to build rapport.

Since his sample was male dominated, and the majority of the young men displayed elements of hegemonic masculinity – expressed primarily through presenting themselves as strong, tough, and fearless (Connell, 2005; Deuchar, 2015) – other forms of impression management became helpful. As referred to elsewhere (Deuchar, 2015), Deuchar's active cultivation of a muscular

46 *Dealing with Boundaries*

physique through bodybuilding, widely respected within the macho circles he was hanging around in, became a tool of 'impression management' and passed on easily decoded messages to the young men that he was able to defend himself in potentially volatile social situations (Winlow et al., 2001; Deuchar, 2015).

The extract below is from Deuchar's interview with one young man, 'Jason' [pseudonym], who was a reforming street gang member in Glasgow. It illustrates the way in which Deuchar occasionally found himself laughing at incidents that young men relayed that he might not otherwise find humorous at all. Following the extract, Deuchar uses this as an illustrative example of how ethnographers often have to carefully consider what they want to disclose and not disclose about their attitudes and values and how they may actively withhold emotional reactions in order to avoid antagonism with somewhat volatile participants in the field.

Illustrative Example 2: Interview with a Glasgow Street Gang Member

RD: What was it that led up to you getting issued with a curfew?
Jason: All the gang fightin' ... I got done with assault for three offensive weapons and a breach

[of the peace].

RD: Was that the time when it was something strange that you had (as a weapon) ...?
Jason: A jar of mussels, aye. *[laughter]*
RD: *[Laughter]* Aye, I remember you told me!

[Joint laughter]

RD: I remember you told me about that. I think that was the most unusual weapon I have heard of. And it was your first offence and you were right away banged up with the curfew?
Jason: Aye.
RD: And that was a year, so that was quite a long time.
Jason: Aye, fuckin' murder, man – a pain in the arse.

'FRONT-STAGE' VS. 'BACK-STAGE' REFLECTIONS BY DEUCHAR

In the above interview with Jason (who was aged 19 at the time), I was exploring his experiences of the justice system, and in particular home detention curfews. During our discussion, Jason made reference to being arrested for assault via the use of a dangerous weapon, which in this case was rather unusual and one that he had referred to in a previous interview with me (Deuchar, 2015). The fact that he had used a jar of mussels as a weapon was something that he evidently viewed as somewhat amusing and so I deliberately prompted him to refer to it again. Even though my natural instinct is to abhor violence of any kind, as an ethnographic interviewer I was determined to create friendly rapport and ensure that I obtained as rich data as possible. In order to do so, I actively encouraged Jason's sense of humour and even laughed at the misdemeanour myself, while also showing some sympathy for the feelings of frustration he felt while on a prolonged curfew.

Here, it is helpful to remind ourselves of Goffman's contention that, learning about the social worlds of offenders often involves the researcher in submitting unconditionally to their company and being open to adopting 'front stage' performances which may differ from their 'back-stage' equivalents. While Jason's perspectives could be described as being diametrically opposed to my own (Drake & Harvey, 2014), where he clearly was amused by his use of a somewhat bizarre weapon to inflict violence on others, I was keen to maintain the egalitarian, trusting relationship that I had earlier established with him (Hewitt, 2007). Fine (1993, p. 271) highlights that the 'illusion of being more sympathetic than we are aids research but is deceptive'. I was, in truth, less sympathetic towards Jason than I led him to believe, but confessing those emotions and becoming judgemental would have limited Jason's candidness and led to weaker and thinner data – or no data at all (Deuchar, 2015) Thus, my approach during interviews with many of the young men I worked with was one where my 'front-stage' performances were very different from my 'back-stage' beliefs and values. This ensured that I 'fitted in' and became accepted as a legitimate - albeit 'marginal' – native of the young men's social landscapes (Deuchar, 2015). At the same time, I regularly found myself reminding them (and myself) about my main role as an academic researcher – thus ensuring that I avoided the risk of going native (Gemignani, 2011).

Covertness and Upholding Ethical Standards

In addition to working extensively with gang members, Deuchar's research has also focussed on the policing of gangs and the related issue of procedural justice within law enforcement on an international basis. As part of a Fulbright scholarship, in 2017 Deuchar's work took him to the USA where he spent approximately 80 hours in the field engaged in participant observation of police practice across two southern counties (Deuchar et al., 2021). During this period, it is true to say that American law enforcement officers were (and still are) finding themselves in the 'social media era of policing' (Shjarback et al., 2017, p. 49), where their actions were (and are) frequently captured on video and quickly uploaded to websites, live-streamed, and viewed by millions. Much of this unprecedented level of public scrutiny combined with the increased politicisation of policing by mass media arose as a result of multiple incidents of deadly force involving officer-involved shootings of, and other forms of violence towards, young black men. Most notably, the lethal shooting of Michael Brown in Ferguson, Missouri in 2014 and (most recently) the killing of George Floyd in Minneapolis in 2020 (for discussion, see Deuchar et al., 2021).

As Deuchar et al. (2021) have argued, the public's consciousness about issues concerning officer prejudice, discrimination and brutality has become heightened within the context of increased news and social media consumption and in an age of digital activism (see also Perry, 2009; Bonilla & Rosa, 2015; Intravia et al., 2018). Some have argued that police are facing a 'major legitimacy crisis' fuelled by a growing 'anti-police sentiment' around the world, but particularly within the USA (MacGuire et al., 2017, p. 739). Officers are more aware of the negative publicity that surrounds policing and mindful of the public's ability to video record their interactions using smartphones (Deuchar et al., 2021), with many believing they are unfairly scrutinised and wish to avoid becoming the star of a career-ending viral video (Davis, 2015; Deuchar, 2021).

The following extract from Deuchar's (2019) fieldnotes illustrates his experience of participating in one of many police deployments with American officers, the majority of whom were White. On this occasion, he accompanied an officer, who was assigned to a county-level unit that focussed primarily on the detection, prevention, and enforcement of gang-related violent crime, as he policed a local community fairground. After asking several young black males to remove gang-affiliated bandanas, the officer apparently felt compelled to approach a young White man. Following the extract, and again writing in the first person, Deuchar uses this as an illustrative example of how, although ethnographers may be open and transparent about their research intentions to their primary empirical participants, a certain amount of covertness may always be necessary. Implications for ethical principles and standards are also discussed.

Illustrative Example 3: Participant Observation of an American Police Deployment

A young black man is walking towards the officers with his girlfriend and I notice he has a red bandana on. The white officer, Sergeant Ryan, immediately approaches him. 'Hey, buddy, take off the bandana' he says firmly. The boy makes to walk away. 'Hey, come here – take it off now', Ryan insists. 'Ok, I'm doin' it,' the boy replies and he quickly slips off the bandana from his head. 'Yeah, you don't want someone bouncing your head tonight – someone sees you with this on and thinks you've got beef it could turn nasty,' Ryan explains. I then notice a young white male approaching, hand in hand with his girlfriend. Like the many young black men the

Sergeant has approached this evening, I notice he is also wearing a bandana. However, this one looks more like a fashion accessory rather than being in any way gang-related. 'Hey, buddy you need to take the bandana off,' Ryan, the Sergeant, says to him. The boy reaches up and slips the bandana off. He looks puzzled, 'Oh, is it gang stuff?' he asks. Ryan nods and the boy seems content with this and walks off. As he does, Ryan turns to me and says, 'yes, he's just a skinny young punk – he's tryin' to look cool in front of his chick, what gang is he in? Maybe a skater gang!' he laughs ironically. 'But you know, I've asked every African American kid in here to take their bandana off so if I don't tell him to do it I'll be accused of being racist,' he says in a very cynical way.

    (Researcher's fieldnotes, adapted from Deuchar et al., 2019)

REFLECTIONS ON 'ETHICAL COVERTNESS' BY DEUCHAR

As we asserted earlier, covert research is not always an 'antithesis' to open and overt research and, even where ethnographers are upfront about their research intentions to those around them, 'a certain amount of covertness' will always be involved in their fieldwork (Deventer, 2009, p. 51).

In engaging in participant observation of American police deployments, I became conscious that I was collecting data in settings over which I had very little control. I recognised that, in addition to observing the behaviour of primary research participants (police officers), in the heat of the police operations I was coming into contact with secondary groups of participants, including young men who were, or suspected to be, gang members. These young men were uninformed about my researcher identity and the nature of the work I was there to do. If the police intervention was relatively low-key in nature and lent itself to informal, prolonged engagement, I was able to introduce these secondary participants to my research and seek their consent to observe their interactions with officers. However, in some cases, the nature of the police interaction was such that any attempt to intervene and seek formal consent from the young men would have been both obtrusive and inappropriate. Thus, these tertiary participants remained unaware of my researcher identity but were observed and became part of my fieldnotes (see also Deuchar, 2015).

The above extract came within the post-Ferguson context of increased tension between American law enforcement and the general public, the increasing galvanisation of the Black Lives Matter (aka BLM) movement and reduced levels of police legitimacy within communities of colour (Deuchar et al., 2021). Some have argued that this contextual backdrop has, on the one hand, increased the public accountability of American policing, while also taking its toll on law enforcement in terms of a growth of fear, cynicism and apprehension and decreased morale amongst officers (Wolfe & Nix, 2016; Torres et al., 2018). As alluded to earlier, as a White male researcher from another country, I was unable to fully and legitimately appreciate neither the full impact of the historical marginalisation and exclusion of people of colour nor the White privilege upheld and enjoyed by the majority of White Americans, and in particular how the latter has manifested itself within American policing. However, I was acutely aware of the potential volatility associated with police/youth encounters within the post-Ferguson era. It would have, therefore, been hugely inappropriate for me to intervene and make my researcher identity and intentions known to the young participants around me during Officer Ryan's interactions with either young Black or White male citizens. Whatever our views on Officer Ryan's reactionary behaviour and dialogue, it was evident to me that the post-Ferguson context had, indeed, had an impact on this and the apparent cynicism of the officer (which I was subsequently able to reflect on further during the write-up of my research findings). However, I had to accept that the process of creating authentic portraits of police interactions and practice had to involve some subtle forms of deception (Fine, 1993; Maszano, 2007; Deuchar, 2015). The tertiary youth participants remained unaware that they were part of my fieldwork observations.

Against the backdrop of the expectations of ethics committees that all participants should give informed consent to being observed, this left me with some dilemmas. As also outlined in wider reflections elsewhere (Deuchar, 2015), I continually sought advice from my primary fieldwork gatekeepers, ethics committee members and colleagues. But, more importantly, I reflected on my own moral and ethical beliefs about how best to maintain an approach to data collection that was situationally ethical (Fine, 1993; Westmarland, 2001; Hammersley & Atkinson, 2007). In the end, I decided to report on the data collected from observations of those young men who were clearly over the age of 18, but ensuring that the real names of participants or even of counties, neighbourhoods, and streets where the fieldwork took place were never mentioned within fieldnotes. Thus, I ensured complete anonymity and avoided harm to all concerned. While participants such as the young men in the above illustration were ultimately unaware that they had been observed by a researcher, I was also convinced that the highest degree of personal ethical and moral standards underpinned the data that finally reached the public domain (Deuchar, 2015).

Conclusion

In this chapter, we have discussed the way in which, as qualitative researchers, we often have to immerse ourselves within the social contexts and lived experiences of our field participants. In comparison to other disciplines, for criminologists this arguably comes with multiple implications and potential risks – and these are heightened further if we adopt an ethnographic approach. We have discussed the need for trust and rapport-building with marginalised and disadvantaged groups who may often be potentially traumatised but also violent; and the need for impression management and the dichotomy between 'front-stage' and 'back-stage' performances (Goffman, 1959; Hammersley & Atkinson, 2007). The risk of 'going native' has been touched upon, and we have explored the balance that is required between being sufficiently involved [with] and being appropriately detached from our research participants (Beyens et al., 2015). As ethnographic criminologists, we have argued that we generally need to accept that some degree of deception and covertness will always exist within our fieldwork. However, it is how we ensure a healthy balance between the need for rigour and the capturing of rich data with the need for upholding ethical principles that is important (Fine, 1993; Hammersley & Atkinson, 1983; Miller, 1995; Calvey, 2013; Deuchar, 2015).

The chapter focussed mainly on providing illustrative examples of how Deuchar, as an ethnographic researcher himself, has attempted to manage the (sometimes 'blurred') boundaries between himself and his research participants. We have discussed the way in which Deuchar's adoption of a 'chameleon-like identity' (Drake & Harvey, 2014, p. 493) enabled him to fluctuate at times between attachment and detachment in order to appreciate and empathise with his (often traumatised) participants while also maintaining his academic identity and credentials. We have also provided insights into the way in which Deuchar sometimes had to adopt 'front stage' performances that were very different from his 'backstage' values as a means of building enough trust with young street gang members that would lend itself to the gathering of rich, authentic data (Goffman, 1959; Drake & Harvey, 2014). Finally, we have illustrated the way in which Deuchar's determination to create authentic portraits of police interaction and practice ultimately involved subtle forms of deception in the form of disguising his identity from those young men that officers interacted with on the streets.

Throughout all of these illustrations, we believe that we have provided sufficient reassurance to readers that, although ethnographic researchers may often find the need to deviate from idealised ethical guidelines, they can still ensure that the highest degree of personal ethical and moral standards underpin their research methods (Deuchar, 2015). In this chapter, we provided examples of the way in which the ethnographer may simultaneously accept the blurring of boundaries with his/her research participants and become a 'marginal native', while also avoiding 'going native' and taking the utmost precautions against any harm coming to his/her participants. However, as Deuchar's experiences illustrate, White, male ethnographers often have to accept their limitations in being able to legitimately appreciate the full impact of the deep-rooted subordination and marginalisation that people of colour have historically experienced. Accordingly, in spite of their need and ability to cross boundaries, in relation to issues of culture and race, some ethnographers may need to accept that their role as an 'outsider' will always be the dominant one during their fieldwork.

52   *Dealing with Boundaries*

References

Beyens, K., Kennes, P., Snacken, S., & Tournel, H. (2015) The craft of doing qualitative research in prisons. *International Journal for Crime, Justice and Social Democracy*, 4(1), 66–78.

Bonilla, Y., & Rosa, J. (2015) #Ferguson: Digital protest, hashtag ethnography, and the racial politics of social media in the United States. *American Ethnologist*, 42(1), 4–1

Bourne, J. (1998) Researchers experience emotions too. In R. S. Barbour & G. Huby (eds.), *Meddling with mythology: AIDS and the social construction of knowledge*. London: Routledge, 90–104.

Calvey, D. (2013) Covert ethnography in criminology: A submerged yet creative tradition. *Current Issues in Criminal Justice*, 25(1), 541–550.

Connell, R. W. (2005) Globalization, imperialism, and masculinities. In M. S. Kimmel, J. Hearn, & R. W. Connell (eds.), *Handbook of studies on men & masculinities*, Thousand Oaks, California: Sage, 71–89.

Connell, R. W. (2020) *Masculinities*. London: Routledge.

Davis, A. (2015) 'YouTube effect' has left police officers under siege, law enforcement leaders say. *The Washington Post*, 8 October. Available at: <https://www.washingtonpost.com/news/post-nation/wp/2015/10/08/youtube-effect-has-leftpolice-officers-under-siege-law-enforcement-leaders-say/>. Last accessed 28 March 2020.

Deuchar, R. (2009) *Gangs, marginalised youth and social capital*. London: Trentham Books.

Deuchar, R. (2015) Dilemmas, deception and ethical decision-making: Insights from a transatlantic ethnographer. In K. Bhopal & R. Deuchar (eds.), *Researching marginalized groups*. New York: Routledge, 78–90.

Deuchar, R. (2018) *Gangs & spirituality: Global perspectives*. Switzerland: Palgrave MacMillan.

Deuchar, R., Crichlow, V. J., & Fallik, S. W. (2019) Cops in crisis?: Ethnographic insights on a new era of politicization, activism, accountability and change in transatlantic policing. *Policing & Society*, 30(1), 47–64.

Deuchar, R., Crichlow, V. J., & Fallik, S. W. (2021) *Police–community relations in times of crisis: Decay and reform in the post-Ferguson Era*. Bristol: Bristol University Press.

Drake, D. H., & Harvey, J. (2014) Performing the role of ethnographer: Processing and managing the emotional dimensions of prison research. *International Journal of Social Research Methodology*, 17(5), 489–501.

Fine, G. A. (1993) Ten lies of ethnography: Moral dilemmas of field research. *Journal of Contemporary Ethnography*, 22(3), 267–294.

Gemignani, M. (2011) Between researcher and researched: An introduction to countertransference in qualitative inquiry. *Qualitative Inquiry*, 17(8), 701–708.

Goffman, E. (1959) *The presentation of self in everyday life*. London: Penguin Books.

Goffman, E. (1961) *Asylums: Essays on the social situation of mental patients and other inmates*. Harmondsworth: Penguin Books.

Gold, R. L. (1958) Roles in sociological field observations. *Social Forces*, 36, 217–223.

Grant, B. M., & Giddings, L. S. (2002) Making sense of methodologies: A paradigm framework for the novice researcher. *Contemporary nurse*, 13(1), 10–28.

Hammersley, M. , & Atkinson, P. (1983) *Ethnography: Principles in practice*. London: Tavistock.

Hammersley, M., & Atkinson, P. (2007) *Ethnography: Principles in practice* (3rd edition). London: Routledge.

Hewitt, J. (2007) Ethical components of researcher—researched relationships in qualitative interviewing. *Qualitative Health Research*, 17(8), 1149–1159.

Intravia, J., Wolff, K., & Piquero, A. (2018) Investigating the effects of media consumption on attitudes toward police legitimacy. *Deviant Behavior*, 39(8), 963–980.

Jensen, S. Q. (2012) 'So, it is about how negative it is?!' Understanding researcher/ researched interactions as relations between intersectional social positions. *Qualitative Studies*, 3(2), 115–132.

Johnstone, G. (2005) Research ethics in criminology. *Research Ethics Review*, 1(2), 60–66.

Maguire, E., Nix, J., & Campbell, B. (2017) A war on cops? The effects of Ferguson on the number of U.S. police officers murdered in the line of duty. *Justice Quarterly*, 35(4), 739–58.

Marzano, M. (2007) Informed consent, deception and research freedom in qualitative research. *Qualitative Inquiry,* 13(3), 417–436.

Miller M (1995) Covert participant observation: Reconsidering the least used method. *Journal of Contemporary Criminal Justice,* 11(2), 97–105.

Perry, B. (2009) Impacts of disparate policing in Indian country. *Policing and Society*, 19(3), 263–81.

Richards, H., & Emslie, C. (2000) The 'doctor' or the 'girl from the university'? Considering the influence of professional roles on qualitative interviewing. *Family Practice,* 17(1), 71–75.

Sharpe, G. (2017) Sociological stalking? Methods, ethics and power in longitudinal criminological research. *Criminology & Criminal Justice*, 17(3), 233–247.

Shjarback J., Pyrooz, D., Wolfe, S., & Decker, S. (2017) De-policing and crime in the wake of Ferguson: Racialized changes in the quality and quality of policing among Missouri police departments. *Journal of Criminal Justice*, 50, 42–52.

Torres, J., Reling, T., & Hawdon, J. (2018) Role conflict and psychological impacts of the post-Ferguson period on law enforcement motivation, cynicism, and apprehensiveness. *Journal of Police and Criminal Psychology*, 33(4), 358–374.

Van Deventer, J. P. (2009) Ethical considerations during human centred overt and covert research. *Quality & Quantity*, 43(1), 45–57.

Villenas, S., & Deyhle, D. (1999) Critical race theory and ethnographies challenging the stereotypes: Latino families, schooling, resilience and resistance. *Curriculum Inquiry*, 29(4), 413–445.

Westmarland, L. (2001) Blowing the whistle on police violence. *British Journal of Criminology,* 41, 523–535.

Winlow, S., Hobbs, D., Lister, S., & Hadfield, P. (2001) Get ready to duc:. Bouncers and the realities of ethnographic research on violent groups. *The British Journal of Criminology*, 41(3), 536–548.

Wolfe, S., & Nix, J. (2016) The alleged 'Ferguson Effect' and police willingness to engage in community partnership. *Law and Human Behavior*, 40(1), 1–10.

Worley, R. M., Worley, V. B., & Wood, B. A. (2016) 'There were ethical dilemmas all day long!': Harrowing tales of ethnographic researchers in criminology and criminal justice. *Criminal Justice Studies*, 29(4), 289–308.

4 Dealing with Research Emotions
Emotional Engagement, Exposure, and Reflexivity

Introduction

Emotional Engagement, Trauma, and Reflexivity

It has been argued that states of emotional arousal, including anger, fear, sadness, and disgust, are deeply implicated in many areas of criminological enquiry (De Haan & Loader, 2002). Inevitably, criminal behaviour itself is often characterised by emotions such as guilt and shame, and yet it is often the case that researchers involved in the study of such behaviour do not pay sufficient attention to their own emotional reactions and states, and how these impact on the research process (Widdowfield, 2000; De Haan & Loader, 2002; Garrighy & Watters, 2020). Drawing on our own experience as criminologists who focus on real-world, interpretivist approaches, we would tend to concur with Fitzpatrick and Olson's (2015) view that emotional engagement is an essential part of conducting qualitative research.

Emotions are a central element in everyday life, and 'fundamental to how we understand ourselves and others' (Fitzpatrick & Olson, 2015, p. 49; see also Denzin, 1984). Empathic connections between ourselves as researchers and those we study enable us to gain richer insights and understanding of participants' experiences. This is particularly the case where sensitive issues are the central focus within an interview context, and nowhere more so within those discussions focussed on participants' motivations for and experiences of criminal behaviour (ibid). Hubbard et al. (2001) argue, for instance, that an emotional outburst during an interview can signal to researchers what is significant (Fitzpatrick & Olson, 2015) – thus enabling the researcher to draw upon 'emotionally-sensed knowledge' to gain greater insight into an interviewee's interpretations. However, it is true to say that methodological texts and University ethics committees often continue to emphasise the need for 'emotional neutrality' in order to minimise the risks of 'going native' or losing a sense of objectivity (Fitzpatrick & Olson, 2015, p. 49).

In direct contrast to these ethical guidelines, we would argue that embracing emotional responses to interviewees is unavoidable and desirable. It is a means of gaining a more 'embodied understanding' of participants' behaviour,

DOI: 10.4324/9781003304746-4

motivations, and experiences (ibid, p. 54). This is particularly the case where ethnographic approaches are drawn upon, and where data is being collected against the backdrop of potentially emotive and violent environments such as prisons and hot-spot crime areas within local communities (Nielsen, 2010; Deuchar, 2015; Deuchar, 2018).

Given the substantial developments in qualitative research over the past four decades, it is somewhat surprising to find how little attention is still paid towards the impact of the researcher's emotions within the qualitative tradition. Widdowfield (2000, p. 200) highlights that there is now common recognition of the way in which a researcher's positionality 'in terms of race, nationality, age, gender, social and economic status, sexuality' may influence the data and the emerging knowledge. And yet, he argues, there is still a proclivity towards what could be described as 'masculinist' knowledge and ways of knowing – whereby discussion of emotions is still assumed to be 'feminine' and even irrelevant to academic scholarship and debate (ibid). Widdowfield argues that there is nothing inherently 'feminist' about recognising the influence of emotions in academic research. On the contrary, Widdowfield highlights that writing emotions into research accounts can not only facilitate a better understanding of the work undertaken but can also provide a 'cathartic unburdening' for the researcher as well as support for other researchers whose work may take them into similarly emotive situations (p. 205).

As authors, our own qualitative criminological research has taken us into the most challenging and triggering situations and contexts, and we ourselves have mostly been the primary research instruments (see, Deuchar, 2009, 2018; Deuchar et al., 2019; Rahman, 2016, 2019; Rahman et al., 2020). Garrihy and Watters (2020, p. 1) make reference to Liebling's (1999) and Jewkes' (2011) appeals to researchers to engage with emotions more substantively within their writing, and in particular for criminologists to consider the subject of emotion from an 'autobiographical perspective'. This is arguably even more important where researchers' fieldwork exposes them to extended discussions on the impact of personal trauma on subsequent offending behaviour (Guerzoni, 2020).

Although as authors we recognise that our research has never been *about us,* we also recognise that the research has been conducted *by us* – as 'emotional agents' (Garrihy & Watters, 2020, p. 1). Accordingly, we believe our data has been co-constructed with our participants, and that our collective emotions have been central to this (ibid). Whereas criminology as a discipline has often been accused of lacking humanity, we believe our willingness to engage emotionally with our participants, fieldwork sites, and emerging data is a key strength within our own academic work. As such, in our published articles and books, autobiographical and confessional narratives often feature, and we suggest that our reflexive approach to coding and analysis of data has been a critical element in protecting ourselves from the effects of secondary trauma that can so easily emerge as a result of the type of fieldwork we have spent our careers engaged in. Quite simply, the adoption of a more reflexive approach to processing emotions has enabled us not only to deepen our understanding of the people and contexts we have studied but also to better process our own feelings and responses to these individuals and situations (Jewkes, 2011).

Nowhere has this been more apparent than within our fieldwork conducted in prisons and with those who have experienced incarceration. Our research participants in these contexts have almost always been the victims of extreme trauma earlier in their lives. Engaging with them for prolonged periods has required significant emotional commitment on our part. Drake and Harvey (2014, p. 497) draw attention to the emotional extremes that characterise a prison environment, where prisoners frequently experience 'fear of violence, self-harm, suicide attempts, unanticipated disturbances or assaults'. They argue that the rapidly changing range of emotions experienced by informants can elicit extreme emotions in researchers.

Building on this, Guerzoni (2020, p. 1) refers to the emergence of 'vicarious trauma', whereby a researcher (or practitioner) becomes 'negatively affected and transformed, over time, consequent to having engaged empathetically with the survivors and accounts of trauma' (see also Moran & Asquith, 2020). Researchers may engage in various forms of emotional labour to manage this trauma, and in the remainder of this chapter, we present illustrative examples of Deuchar's experiences while working with reformed and reforming gang members and members of OCGs, all of whom had suffered extreme trauma. In sharing the emotional responses that Deuchar experienced and the way in which he actively and reflexively engaged with these responses, we hope that we will be able to support and inform the work of others who are engaged in similar fieldwork (Jewkes, 2011; Fitzpatrick & Olson, 2015).

Tales from the Field: Illustrative Examples and Reflexive Accounts Engaging with Personal Emotions from an Autobiographical Stance

In addition to his work on street gangs in Los Angeles and Glasgow, Deuchar's international ethnographic research also allowed him to explore potential vehicles and enablers for desistance among motorcycle gang members and members of OCGs in Denmark (see Deuchar, 2018). He travelled there on several occasions to explore the potential impact of ascetic-spiritual practices such as yoga and meditation in prisons and in the community and their potential for enhancing positive psychological states among former male members of these groups. In particular, his work focussed on the use of Sadarshan Kryia Yoga (SKY), which has been described as a 'sequence of specific breathing techniques' (Brown & Gerbarg, 2005, p. 189) and an example of 'indigenous Hindu spirituality' (Pandya, 2016, p. 134). Its use is coordinated by the *Art of*

Living Foundation, a nonprofit service organisation founded in 1982 by the spiritual Indian leader Sri Sri Ravi Shankar (Vedamurthachar et al., 2006).

SKY comprises four components, all conducted in a sitting posture: three-stage slow Ujjayi pranayama, consisting of slow-deep breathing; Bhastrika pranayama, consisting of forced inhalation and exhalation twenty times; chanting of 'om'; and Sudarshan Kriya, a process consisting of slow, medium, and fast cycles of breathing practised for a total duration of around 30 minutes (Vedamurthachar et al. 2006). Variations of the techniques are used in many traditions including Raja yoga, Hatha yoga and Zen, and can be combined with physical yoga stretches and meditation (Brown & Gerbarg, 2005; Deuchar, 2018).

The *Breathe Smart* programme was founded in Denmark in 2000, with the specific goal of teaching and coaching participants to use SKY as a means of potentially supporting them to deal with challenging life circumstances (*Breathe Smart*, 2016). Its partner programme, *Prison Smart*, is focussed specifically on supporting prison inmates to address the same issues (*Breathe Smart*, 2016). Both programmes draw upon a traditional model of SKY that combines the use of Ujjayi pranayama, Bhastrika pranayama and Sudarshan Kriya as per the teachings of Sri Sri Ravi Shankar and promoted globally by the *Art of Living Foundation* (Brown & Gerbarg 2005; Vedamurthachar et al., 2006; Pandya, 2016; Deuchar, 2018).

Throughout 2016-18, Deuchar conducted semi-structured interviews and engaged in wider, informal discussions with a sample of 25 Danish men with former involvement in violent and drug-related criminality associated with motorcycle gang membership and/or who had been members of OCGs. While some of the men were in prison when interviewed, others had recently been released back into the community. The following extract from Deuchar's (2018) fieldnotes illustrates some of the insights he gained from interviews and informal conversations with the men as well as his own experience of participating in the SKY programme himself, guided by coaches from *Breathe Smart*. Following the extract, and (as in the previous chapter) writing in the first person, Deuchar uses this as an illustrative example of how ethnographers like ourselves benefit from reflecting on our own emotional responses in the field.

Illustrative Example 1: Participant Observation Within the 'Breathe Smart' Programme [Source: Deuchar, 2018]

The men talked about their initial reactions to the yoga movements, forced inhalation, and cycled breathing techniques that they experienced on the initial five-day programme and the progressive impact they felt from practising the techniques on their own afterwards. Some described an initial frustration with the presence of the Sudarshan Kriya mantra that was played on a tape while they practised, or admitted that they found the physical yoga exercises tough.

However, they also made reference to feelings of psychological release that, in some cases led to a clarity of mind or even intense emotional responses:

> The first time I did this I was so angry that I wanted to like to go up and go out of the room or even smash the ghetto blaster where this guy was saying 'so ... om' ... but I was like, something else tell me 'no, you've got to stay, you've got to see what this is because you're scared, there's something you're scared about.' Afterwards, I could feel some release in my brain actually.
>
> (Ivan)

> The first day I took the course ... it was OK. And the second day it was Ok, and then the day came we had to do the Sudarshan Kriya for the first time, the breathing ... and when I get home and I get inside the door, you know, I sat in my kitchen for a while and I [was] then just crying ... it was really looking into myself for the first time in my life, and see all the fucked-up things I've been doing.
>
> (Lucas)

Through personal experience of participating in the Kryia, I realised the way in which it could initially feel strange or frustrating, but in a short time led to feelings of intense psychological and physical release:

> Haggi switches on the tape, and I am completely unprepared for what comes next. As I listen, sitting in the chair with my hands on my lap, I am guided by a high pitched, Hindu voice which repeats a mantra over the loud speaker. At first the mantra is slow and the corresponding breaths by nature are deep and relaxed, but after several minutes the pace quickens and the breaths then also speed up – until they are shallow and guided with some urgency. Following this, the mantra slows again and the quick intakes of breathe slow down in pace. I don't feel in my comfort zone, but I decide to stick with it ... After what feels like about 20 minutes I am completely carried away with the pace and form of the breathing and the mantra until I feel my head becoming light and the knot in my stomach subsiding.
>
> (Researcher's fieldnotes)

Other men in the sample also talked about the way in which the yoga, breathing, and meditation exercises provided them with a tool that enabled them to manage their aggression and anger and deal with potentially destructive thoughts, feelings, and stressful situations more productively. Some also talked about the intense feelings of happiness and joy that they began to experience after practising the SKY techniques for some time:

Some people cry but I get gladness in me, you know, it's a good feeling. So when I get out of there I'm positive, you know, I'm on like drugs but in a good way and I'm pumped up ... I get this, you know, strong energy, yeah a lot of energy.

(Jamaal)

There's happiness, but it's a peaceful thing and ... when you have done this thing, everything else feels and looks different, you know?

(Lasse)

Indeed, my own personal experience of the practices quickly led me to experience the type of energy, joy, and peace that the men described during interviews:

When the Kriya practice has concluded, I realise that I cannot stop smiling – I feel a great joy, a peaceful presence that surpasses anything I have experienced before either in meditation or in real-time. Slowly, I am beginning to understand why the transformations that the offenders I have been talking to have been happening. If my stress and anxiety can be relieved through this, it is highly likely that their anger and aggression will also be impacted positively by it.

(Researcher's fieldnotes)

SHARED EMOTIONAL REACTIONS TO ASCETIC-SPIRITUAL PRACTICES:
REFLECTIONS BY DEUCHAR

Throughout the initial fieldwork conducted for the above research, my regular visits to Denmark coincided with my own personal experiences of grief. Several months prior to going out into the field, I had lost my father after a long illness. While collecting the first tranche of data in the field (from which the fieldnotes above emerged), my experiences of interviewing research participants while also participating in the breathing and meditation programme were emotionally charged.

Looking back at this period in my personal and professional life, I recognise that participating in the *Breathe Smart* programme elicited emotional arousal within me, as the intense anxiety I had been experiencing for several months as a result of bereavement began to subside for the first time (De Haan & Loader, 2002). This first-hand 'emotionally sensed knowledge' (Fitzpatrick & Olson, 2015, p. 50) of the positive impact of the breathing and meditation programme enabled me to gain a deep empathetic understanding of the emotional responses that my participants had experienced. Quite simply, I related to the ex-offenders' descriptions of their own emotional reactions to the practices (including initial anger and frustration followed by release, happiness, peace, and joy) because I was experiencing them myself.

Reflecting the advice from Liebling (1999) and Jewkes (2011), in constructing fieldnote observations from the research during the long evenings and weekends following the initial data collection, I made the decision to actively engage with my emotions more substantively from an autobiographical stance. Using a reflexive approach, I made reference to the way in which I noticed my personal feelings of anxiety subsiding as a result of the breathing practices and my personal experience of finding 'great joy, a peaceful presence' while participating in the practices.

On the one hand, this enabled me to understand and relate to the way in which the programme may be having a positive impact on the former motorcycle gang members I was interviewing. On the other, it allowed me to focus on the positive aspects of their personal rehabilitation journeys that they described to me while also reducing the potential impact of vicarious trauma that had the potential to emerge while listening empathetically to the men's accounts of the multiple forms of trauma they had experienced during both their formative years and the years they had spent in the gang lifestyle (Guerzoni (2020); Moran & Asquith, 2020).

Exposure to an Outpouring of Emotions during Interviews in Prisons

Throughout 2019 and early 2020, Deuchar brought his fieldwork back to Scotland and embarked on a new qualitative research study that aimed to capture the lived experiences of drug addiction and mental ill-health among men in Scottish prisons. During many months of intermittent visits to two adult prisons, he conducted a series of life history interviews with a sample of incarcerated men that explored the triggers and motivations for, and the nature and extent of, illicit drug misuse among them and the overlap with mental health issues. The study sought to understand the antecedents of drug use and misuse, offenders' motivations for continued drug use in prison, the type of substances most commonly used and their psycho-social consequences, as well as prisoners' views on the provision of mental health and addiction treatment in prison (Deuchar & Densley, 2023).

To be eligible to participate in this study, men aged 21–65 had to be formally recognised as adult prisoners with prior and/or current involvement in illicit drug misuse, and they had to have been incarcerated (on this occasion) for at least one year. In relation to the former criterion, identified gatekeepers, who were trusted sources of support to the men [such as prison chaplains and volunteers who ran drug recovery groups], were able to verify those men who were known to be either currently using substances in prison or who had previously used them (Deuchar & Densley, 2023).

From August 2019 until the closure of Scottish prisons to outsiders owing to the global coronavirus disease 2019 pandemic in March 2020, Deuchar visited both prisons on multiple occasions, initially to meet with those who had indicated an initial willingness to participate in the study. He spent some time building rapport with the men, providing them with the opportunity to ask any questions about the research.

In the end, 24 men agreed to participate in interviews across the two prison estates, each of whom was serving sentences anywhere from 12 months to life imprisonment [mean length = 4.5 years]. The youngest participant was 23 and the oldest was 62 [mean age: 35]. All participants were white. All of the men had served at least one prior prison term, and some were back in prison after being recalled for reoffending and/or missing allocated rehabilitation appointments that were part of their release conditions. Since both prison sites housed a range of short-term, longer-term and life sentence prisoners, samples from both estates had a similar range of ages and incarceration lengths. Thirteen of the 24 interviewees were from Glasgow, Scotland's largest city; eight came from large towns located on the wider west coast of Scotland, either bordering or geographically close to Glasgow; and three participants were from other central Scottish cities. The information gathered through interviews was treated in a confidential manner and interviewees were informed of this (Deuchar & Densley, 2023).

The following section provides some key extracts from some of the interviews (as reported in Deuchar & Densley, 2023), where the men often opened up emotionally about their adverse childhood experiences (ACEs) and experiences of trauma that had first stimulated their illegal drug use; their motivations for and experiences with using drugs in prison; and their reflections on the overlap between their drug misuse and mental ill-health, as well as their perceptions of the lack of support available within the prison system for mental health.

Illustrative Example 2: Drug use and Mental Health Issues among Men in Prison [source: Deuchar & Densley, 2023]

Each and every participant in the study described growing up amid poverty and social inequality with exposure to a multiplicity of ACEs, including physical and emotional abuse and neglect, domestic violence, household dysfunction, substance abuse at home, parental separation, and having family members with an incarceration history. Some men also talked about suffering from father absence and/or being aware of family members' involvement in criminality during their formative years:

> My mum took drugs and I ended up goin' to live wi' my gran and grandad when I was four ... my mum died when I was 10 and things just changed from there ... drugs and stuff. – Ben, age 29
>
> (prison two)

> I lived with my mum and my step-dad. Never really got to know my dad. He moved away ... my stepdad started abusing' me, no' sexually but

physically abusin' me ... it was as if it was normality ... I associate that wi' a lot of the anger ... I was always fightin' in school, and getting' suspended n'things. – Danny, age 28

(prison one)

I've got a family full of criminals ... shoplifters, bank robbers, pick pockets, till dippers, drug dealers, gangsters ... at aged 9 or 10 I started becomin' aware of it ... my dad was a binge drinker, a lot of my uncles and aunts used drugs regularly recreationally, social settings. I started noticin' that, the smell of cannabis ... I started to use it myself when I was about 10 or 11. – Rory, age 46

(prison two)

Against this backdrop, interviewees experimented with drugs at an early age, which, they argued, facilitated other forms of offending:

A lot of my teens, I started takin' like ecstasy, valium. Then when I left school n'that, I ended up oot myself, I started using like heroin [at age 15/16] ... it was just the thing that [me and the boys] done ... there was a big change in like my offending n'that. – Charlie, age 38

(prison one)

I had a joint of cannabis when I was about 12. I just happened to be somewhere when it was gettin' passed around. It was New Year's Eve when it occurred. As time went on, I got involved in harder drugs ... I was takin' LSD and amphetamines. When I started gettin' older, I started takin' heroin and cocaine, crack ... it had a serious impact. I started committin' crime to fund my habit. – Jack, age 51

(prison one)

Drug use and dependency preceded prison time for all 24 of the interviewees. Cammy (aged 42, prison two), for example, had a long history of cannabis use, followed by heroin and benzodiazepines in the community. His drug use got worse in prison, however, because drugs were his only 'release' from the monotony of prison life, he said. Similarly, Richie (aged 39, prison one) had used cannabis from the age of 16 and cocaine since he was 18. He drew attention to the fact that prison was not a 'normal environment' so he used drugs inside as a 'coping mechanism ... it blocks out maybe previous thoughts or past things that have happened to [prisoners] in their life'.

Many of the men in the sample felt unsafe in prison and they referenced a dangerous, 'hypermasculine' prison culture that forced them to wear a metaphorical 'mask' and project a false identity simply to navigate contested spaces. Drug use was for them a way to manage the constant associated feelings of tension, anxiety, and stress:

> You need to survive in here ... there's 46 bodies in my section, so I've got 46 faces and different personalities I need to put on for different people ... so you're never really 100% settled because you're always on your toes. – Richie, age 39
>
> (prison one)

> Sometimes I sit in my cell and I'm always feelin' anxious ... I'll use drugs to take that nervousness away ... I wasnae like that before I came to prison ... it's just being in prison just takes all your confidence away. It's just so stressful being in prison. – Ryan, age 41
>
> (prison two)

Many of the men disclosed that they had suffered from various types of neuroses, including phobias, PTSD, and reactive depression (arising as a result of an internal response to an external situation), and in some cases, psychoses such as schizophrenia. The majority admitted that their symptoms had worsened during incarceration. Among those who had reached out for medical and psychological help, it was common for them to describe a lack of available support to help treat their symptoms. Interviewees talked of broken promises of treatment and referrals unfulfilled, stigmatization from medical staff, and being taken off medication that provided them with some psychological respite without warning:

> I break doon two or three times every day ... the last time I seen somebody for mental health, they were like that, 'oh. we're gonna maybe get somebody from Psychology or somethin' to see you,' you know? But I've never heard anythin' aboot that, you know? And I've told them, like what are the main issues ... depression, anxiety n'all that ... but they go, 'oh, all he wants is medication.' That's the way they look at it, know what I mean? ... the first time I've used heroin since last year was last night ... [because] they've took me off my medication ... gabapentin ... I need to try and sleep. – Fraser, age 43
>
> (prison one)

Fraser (above) described being prescribed the anticonvulsant gabapentin to treat his anxiety and the chronic pain he suffered after a difficult surgery he survived when he was younger. Once gabapentin was removed from his prescription, however, Fraser turned to heroin simply to get better sleep, and he was not the only interviewee to imply that prison indirectly initiated their heroin use. For example:

I got my first sentence in 2012 and started takin' subbie [buprenorphine, commonly known by the tradename 'subutex': a mixed opiod agonist-antagonist that helps to prevent withdrawal symptoms caused by stopping other opiates]. So when I was released I had a habit wi' subbie … I remember someone saying, 'take a line of this' and it was heroin. It took the pain away, the way I was feelin'. So I ended up stuck on heroin … the subbie causes the same withdrawals as heroin, so basically me coming to the jail gave me a heroin habit. From the subbie in the halls. – Ben, age 29

(prison two)

Another interviewee, Lewis, started using NPS following multiple suicide attempts and the prison's failure to meet his mental health needs. Daryl similarly began 'self-medicating' on new or novel psychoactive substances (NPS) (formerly known as 'legal highs' or designer/synthetic drugs: analogues of existing controlled drugs or newly synthesised chemicals created to mimic their effects [Shafi et al., 2020]). This was after Lewis admitted feeling suicidal to the doctor but received little medical intervention:

I've had sertraline and stuff, anti-depressant-wise but it never really helps … I've had numerous suicide attempts … I've put in umpteem [multiple] forms for mental health [treatment], but I'm still waitin' …. – Lewis, age 27

(prison two)

I said [to the Doctor] last time that I was feelin' suicidal. They put me on observation, where they come and look through your door every hour and ask if you're alright … they never gave me any medication … I've been self-medicatin' on legal highs … I wanted to stop but I'm strugglin' to stop because I canny sleep at night … I start … feelin' suicidal if I can't sleep properly. – Daryl, age 26

(prison two)

Joel summed up the dual presence of multiple mental health issues in prison halls and the tendency for the men not to open up about this due to the hyper-masculine prison culture but simply to use drugs to self-medicate:

There's a lot of cunts in the jail wi' mental health [issues] … but they're no' really wantin' to come out and speak about it … [so they] just take drugs n'shit. – Joel, age 23

(prison one)

Accordingly, the men found themselves caught in a vicious cycle. On the one hand, they used drugs to self-medicate the symptoms of mental ill-health. On the other hand, using drugs was making their mental health worse.

MANAGING EMOTIONAL AROUSAL AND AVOIDING VICARIOUS
TRAUMA: REFLECTIONS BY DEUCHAR

Having suffered from ACEs that subsequently stimulated extreme trauma and the onset of drug use and offending at young ages, it was evident that the men that I worked with in Scottish prisons had entered the prison system with a wide range of existing vulnerabilities (Maruna & Liebling, 2005). During my extended discussions with them, the men voiced recurring feelings of anxiety and depression, alongside pressure to keep up appearances within the 'hyper-masculine' prison setting (Jewkes, 2005). Continued and, in many cases, accelerated drug use was for many interviewees their only available coping mechanism. The insights from the interviewees appeared to underline those made in earlier research that suggested that (mental) healthcare provision in prisons is inadequate, in part because 'social control' and prison security take precedence over addiction and mental health treatment (Reed & Lynne, 1997; British Medical Association, 2001; Birmingham, 2003; Hughes, 2003; Dolan et al., 2007; Enggist et al., 2014; Deuchar & Densley, 2023).

Accordingly, there was many emotional reflections (such as those outlined above by men like Ben, Lewis, and Daryl) on the way in which the men literally self-medicated on heroin or on NPS in the absence of any form of adequate mental health support. It has been reported that synthetic cannabinoids are generally the most commonly used NPS in prison (Carnie et al., 2017), and in 2014–2015, the synthetic cannabinoid 'Spice' specifically was a concern in over 60% of men's prisons inspected in England and Wales (Ford & Berg, 2018). Kirby (2016, p. 53) refers to an NPS 'epidemic' sweeping through prisons that 'has left prison officers and managers reeling' as they struggle to get to grips with the multiplicity of problems that these new and abundant drugs are causing, most commonly an increased prevalence of mental ill-health (see also Deuchar & Densley, 2023).

As a researcher, conducting the interviews for this particular project was possibly one of the most challenging experiences I have had during a 20+ year career in Higher Education. Spending prolonged periods of time in the Scottish prisons opened up my exposure to and awareness of the emotional extremes that often characterise the prison environment (Drake & Harvey, 2014). The men not only poured out their emotions regarding childhood trauma but also while sharing their previous experiences of self-harm and suicide attempts, their frustrations regarding a lack of mental health support and their desperate attempts to manage their own mental ill-health through self-medication.

Earlier in the chapter, we made reference to Guerzoni's (2020, p. 1) reflections on the possible emergence of 'vicarious trauma', whereby a researcher may become 'negatively affected and transformed, over time, consequent to having engaged empathetically with the survivors and accounts of trauma'. It has been argued that researchers may engage in various forms of emotional labour to manage this trauma; for instance, 'surface acting' may involve altering their behaviour to give the appearance of favourable emotions to others, while 'deep acting' may focus on altering their composition through drawing on practical means of emotional regulation (for discussion, see Guerzoni, 2020, p. 6). During the fieldwork I conducted in Scottish prisons, I believe that my relaxed and empathetic approach encouraged the men to open up to me in great depth about their experiences of trauma and their deep-rooted emotional reactions to the pains of imprisonment (Sykes, 1958). However, at times I found their described experiences and emotional reactions upsetting, and at a certain point in the fieldwork I recognised that the fieldwork was taking its toll on me emotionally.

While both conducting and later transcribing the interviews and analysing the emerging themes, I therefore actively adopted a reflexive approach where I regularly reflected on my own emotional responses and positionality in relation to the men's narratives through personal journaling. When the pandemic emerged and the first national lockdown came into force in March 2020, I also actively used the time to create a number of short video insights for social media, where I reflected on the men's experiences, my own reactions and what I believed needed to change in terms of drug policy and health care in the prison environment. This included, for example, the use of counselling on drug-related issues, the widening use of drug recovery cafés, the housing of drug-using prisoners in specialised units with a treatment approach and wrap-around care and integrated health packages (Deuchar & Densley, 2023).

I found both the journaling and the creation of video reflections shared with my social media followers were cathartic (Moran & Asquith, 2020). These measures did not eliminate the emotional arousal I experienced, and I would argue that this should never be the case since engagement with personal emotions is an essential part of the fieldwork process in criminological, qualitative research. However, I do believe that the approaches I used did ultimately reduce the impact of vicarious trauma by enabling me to better process and regulate the feelings and personal responses to the incarcerated men and the deeply troubling situations and emotions they shared so candidly with me (Jewkes, 2011; Moran & Asquith, 2020).

Conclusion

In this chapter, we have placed the spotlight on the emotional labour that so often is an inherent part of qualitative, criminological research. We have argued that engagement with our own emotions is an essential element in this type of research and that doing so enables us to gain a deeper, more embodied understanding of our research participants' experiences and behaviour (Fitzpatrick & Olson, 2015). Contrary to the commonly held views of ethics committees who often emphasise the need for emotional neutrality, we have drawn attention to the benefits that come when we engage with our own emotions as researchers while out in the field (Liebling, 1999).

In the main body of the chapter, we provided illustrative examples of how Deuchar has used a reflexive approach while engaged in working with reformed or reforming gang members, members of OCGs and men in prison – all of whom opened up to him emotionally during interviews and while reflecting on their personal experiences of trauma. We have illustrated the way in which using fieldnotes, journaling and video contemplations was deeply cathartic (Moran & Asquith, 2020). Not only did it allow Deuchar to process his own emotions responses to the lived experiences of his research participants, but it also helped to protect him from the full impact of vicarious trauma.

Pearlman and Caringi (2009, p. 202) define vicarious trauma as 'the negative transformation in the helper that results from empathic engagement with trauma survivors and their trauma material, combined with a commitment or responsibility to help them'. Further, Moran & Asquith (2020) argue that a key factor that influences the impact of vicarious trauma is empathy. We strongly believe that potential exposure to vicarious trauma during criminological fieldwork is a reflection of the researcher's ability to develop deep empathic connections with his/her participants and with the data and the stories held within the data (Moran & Asquith, 2020). The fact that it had the capacity to emerge during our own empirical work is therefore a positive, since it reflects the depth of trust and connection that was built with research participants. However, we also believe that reflexivity in the research process is essential as a means of deepening the researcher's engagement with the data while also acting as a protective factor to the researcher during deep immersion with trauma survivors in the field.

References

Birmingham, L. (2003) The mental health of prisoners. *Advances in Psychiatric Treatment*, 9(3), 191–199.

Breathe Smart. (2016) Available at: <http://www.breathesmart.co.uk/>. Last accessed 4 September 2023.

British Medical Association (2001) *Prison medicine: A crisis waiting to break*. London: British Medical Association.

Brown, R. P., & Gerbarg, P. L. (2005) Sudarshan Kriya yogic breathing in the treatment of stress, anxiety, and depression: Part I neurophysiologic model. *The Journal of Alternative and Complementary Medicine*, 11(1), 189–201.

Carnie, J., Broderick, R., Cameron, J., Downie, D., & Williams, G. (2017) *Prisoner survey 2017*. Polmont: Scottish Prison Service.

De Haan, W., & Loader, I. (2002) On the emotions of crime, punishment and social control. *Theoretical Criminology*, 6(3), 243–253.

Denzin, N. (1984) *On understanding emotion*. San Francisco, CA: Jossey- Bass.

Deuchar, R. (2009) *Gangs, marginalised youth and social capital*. London: Trentham Books.

Deuchar, R. (2015) Dilemmas, deception and ethical decision-making: Insights from a transatlantic ethnographer. In K. Bhopal & R. Deuchar (eds.), *Researching marginalized groups*. New York: Routledge, 78–90.

Deuchar, R. (2018) *Gangs & spirituality: Global perspectives*. Switzerland: Palgrave MacMillan.

Deuchar, R., Crichlow, V. J., & Fallik, S. W. (2019) Cops in crisis?: Ethnographic insights on a new era of politicization, activism, accountability and change in transatlantic policing. *Policing and Society*, 30(1) 47–64.

Deuchar, R., & Densley, J. (2023) Exploring the intersection of drug addiction and mental ill-health in Scottish prisons: A qualitative study of incarcerated men. *Journal of Drug Issues*. doi: 10.1177/00220426231161282.

Dolan, K., Khoei, E. M., Brentari, C., & Stevens, A. (2007) *Prisons and drugs: A global review of incarceration, drug use and drug services. Report 12*. Beckley Foundation: Drug Policy Programme.

Drake, D. H., & Harvey, J. (2014) Performing the role of ethnographer: Processing and managing the emotional dimensions of prison research. *International Journal of Social Research Methodology*, 17(5), 489–501.

Enggist, S., Møller, L., Galea, G., & Udesen, C. (2014) *Prisons and health*. Copenhagen: World Health Organisation.

Fitzpatrick, P., & Olson, R. E. (2015) A rough road map to reflexivity in qualitative research into emotions. *Emotion Review*, 7(1), 49–54.

Ford, L. T., & Berg, J. D. (2018) Analytical evidence to show letters impregnated with novel psychoactive substances are a means of getting drugs to inmates within the UK prison service. *Annals of Clinical Biochemistry*, 55(6), 673–678.

Garrihy, J., & Watters, A. (2020) Emotions and agency in prison research. *Methodological Innovations*, 13(2), 1–14.

Guerzoni, M. A. (2020) Vicarious trauma and emotional labour in researching child sexual abuse and child protection: A postdoctoral reflection. *Methodological Innovations*, 13(2), 1–8.

Hubbard, G., Backett-Milburn, K., & Klemmer, D. (2001) Working with emotion: Issues for the researcher in fieldwork and teamwork. *International Journal of Social Research Methodology*, 4, 119–137.

Hughes, R. (2003) Drugs, prisons and harm reduction. *Journal of Health and Social Policy*, 18(2), 43–54.

Jewkes, Y. (2005) Men behind bars: 'Doing' masculinity as an adaptation to imprisonment. *Men and Masculinities*, 8(1), 44–63.

Jewkes, Y. (2011) Autoethnography and emotion as intellectual resources: Doing prison research differently. *Qualitative Inquiry*, 18(1), 63–75.

Kirby, T. (2016) New Psychoactive Substances in prisons: High and getting higher. *Insight*, 3, 709–710.

Liebling, A. (1999) Doing research in prison: Breaking the silence? *Theoretical Criminology*, 3(2), 147–173.

Maruna, S., & Liebling, A. (2005) *The effects of imprisonment*. Cullompton: Willan.

Moran, R. J., & Asquith, N. L. (2020) Understanding the vicarious trauma and emotional labour of criminological research. *Methodological Innovations*, 13(2). doi: 10.1177/2059799120926085.

Nielsen, M. M. (2010) Pains and possibilities in prison: On the use of emotions and positioning in ethnographic research. *Acta Sociologica*, 53(4), 307–321.

Pandya, A. P. (2016) Sudarshan Kriya of the art of living foundation: Applications to social work practice. *Practice: Social Work in Action,* 28(2), 133–154.

Pearlman, L. A., & Caringi, J. (2009) Living and working self-reflectively to address vicarious trauma. In C. A. Courtois & J. D. Ford (eds.), *Treating complex traumatic stress disorders: An evidence-based guide.* New York: Guilford Press, 202–224.

Rahman, M. (2016) Understanding organised crime and fatal violence in Birmingham: A case study of the 2003 new year shootings. Papers from the British Criminology Conference, Vol 16.

Rahman, M. (2019) *Homicide and organised crime: Ethnographic narratives of serious violence in the criminal underworld.* London: Palgrave.

Rahman, M., McLean, R., Deuchar, R., & Densley, J. (2020) Who are the enforcers? The motives and methods of muscle for hire in West Scotland and the West Midlands. *Trends in Organized Crime,* 25(1), 108–129.

Reed, J., & Lyne, M. (1997) The quality of healthcare in prison: Results of a year's programme of semi-structured inspections. *BMJ,* 315, 1420–1424.

Shafi, A., Berry, A. J., Sumnall, H., Wood, D. M., & Tracy, D. K. (2020) New psychoactive substances: A review and updates. *Therapeutic Advances in Psychopharmacology,* 10. doi: 10.1177/2045125320967197.

Sykes, G. M. (1958) *The society of captives.* Princeton, NJ: Princeton University Press.

Vedamurthachar, A., Janakiramaiah, N., Hegde, J. M., Shetty, T. K., Subbakrishna, D. K., Sureshbabu, S. V., & Gangadhar, B. N. (2006) Antidepressant efficacy and hormonal effects of Sudarshana Kriya Yoga (SKY) in alcohol dependent individuals. *Journal of Affective Disorders,* 94, 249–253.

Widdowfield, R. (2000) The place of emotions in academic research. *Area,* 32(2), 199–208.

5 Research Publication, the Future of Research Ethics, and Practical Recommendations

Introduction

Research Publication

This section offers brief albeit important information on the ethical publication of research. It emphasises the importance of meeting the needs of readers, transparency, plagiarism, citation practices, authorship, peer-review, and open access publishing.

1. **Meeting the needs of readers:** Most academic work is published in academic journals, books, or dissertations. Some aspects of academic work can also be published as grey literature, which tend to be outputs that are not produced by commercial publishers. These publication types include reports, working papers, government documents, white papers, and evaluations. Researchers should have a clear understanding of where they intend to publish prior to commencing a study, as considering this from the outset can help them to write to the publisher's specifications and audience. For example, scholars in criminology and wider social sciences that publish academically, either publish through a journal article or a book. These two modes of scholarly publishing are usually peer-reviewed, rigorous, and time consuming. However, both also differ in relation to the needs of their readers.

   Academic journals often target a smaller audience in comparison to academic books. This is because journals often target a specialised audience within a particular field of study who are often seeking to acquire knowledge that is concise, focused, and empirically driven information that either introduces or contributes to an ongoing scientific discussion. Books, on the other hand, like this one, for instance, tend to target a broader audience, including students, educators, practitioners, as well as general readers that have a vested interest in gaining a deeper understanding of a topic. By design and length, books often provide more coverage, context, and mixture of information compared to journal articles. This allows them to incorporate various writing styles and formats,

DOI: 10.4324/9781003304746-5

thus making them versatile in encompassing narratives, case studies, and illustrative examples to engage and educate a diverse readership beyond the confines of academic discourse.

Prior to deciding where to publish and what format, researchers should consider the following questions:

- Who are my intended readers?
- What are their needs and how can they be met?
- What platforms can they access information?
- How do they engage with content?
- What are their expectations?

2. **Transparency:** The understanding of transparency has been alluded to in previous chapters, especially when discussing the acquisition of research ethical approval in chapter two. When publishing academic research, authors should include detailed reporting of methods and results, acknowledgement of study limitations and mitigation of biases, all of which are vital for scientific integrity and disciplinary progress. The transparent reporting of methods and findings also allows other researchers to verify and replicate the findings of the study, thus ensuring research reliability and validity.

   Transparent reporting in research also facilitates the legacy of knowledge over time, reinforces ethical conduct by preventing the misrepresentation or manipulation of datasets and bias mitigation. From a disciplinary standpoint, it fosters a culture of openness, accountability, rigour, reliability, and the advancement of scientific impact through research for the benefit of society.

3. **Plagiarism:** A major academic misconduct in research is plagiarism, which we define as the act to copy a person's work. Even if that work has been rephrased irrespective of the approach and without any personal contribution, it is a violation of academic integrity. Unfortunately, plagiarism is a thorny issue in academic publishing, and publisher's often accept the work of researchers on trust. Important here is to recognise that there are serious consequences often associated with plagiarism for researchers and their institutions, often resulting in academic misconduct. As such, it is paramount for researchers to ensure that any published work is theirs, guaranteeing that any secondary information within their work is textually evidenced appropriately.

4. **Citation practices:** The adequate evidencing of information often through referencing is crucial for not only highlighting previous contributions but also demonstrating integrity and avoiding plagiarism in your own work. The citation style may vary across disciplines and publishers; thus, researchers should familiarise themselves with citation guidelines to promote consistency and uphold ethical precepts. If researchers are

required to cite contentious or disputed sources that may fall within the remit of grey literature, caution is required, particularly in cases where there is a blur between common ideas or original knowledge.

5. **Authorship:** For students carrying out research projects like dissertations or a PhD, authorship tends to not be an issue. However, for research that is carried out collaboratively, it is ethically important to ensure that individuals who have made contributions are appropriately recognised as authors. Recognising collaborator contributions involves the acknowledgement of specific duties and responsibilities, whether in idea conception, study design, data collection, analysis, writing and overall project management. If responsibilities are not clarified at the beginning of a project and not reviewed through the course of the project, disputes may occur in relation to authorship order for the final publication. We believe that most authorship disputes can be resolved through transparent communication and effective dialogue primarily between the authors. If this fails, resolving any disagreements may then require the input of institutional bodies such as the ethics committee that approved the research or the publisher. The ethical achievement of authorship by default fosters mutual respect among peers, trust, and accountability. By adhering to these principles, researchers promote fairness, transparency, and collegiality in collaborative outputs.

Research Ethics in a World of Artificial Intelligence

The use of technology in research has not only altered the way that we make sense of the world but has also transformed our experiences of how we do so. Within the social sciences, one of the persistent polarities is apparent in rationalism and empiricism (Bernard, 2000; Bryman, 2016). Rationalism is often viewed to be knowledge derived from logic and reason, whereas empiricism is achieved from experience and experimentation. As scholars that primarily engage in qualitative inquiries, namely ethnography and case-based research, we have both heavily gravitated towards studies that originate from The Chicago School. Most of the studies played a tremendous role in encouraging the development of empiricism, largely specialising in the urban sociology of criminological subjects (Park, 1915; Anderson, 1923; Thrasher, 1927; Wirth, 1928; Zorbaugh, 1929). Robert E. Park, an eminent Chicago School scholar stated the below to his students, which was observed by Howard Becker, and later published in print by McKinney (1966, p. 71):

> You have been told to go grubbing in the library, thereby accumulating a mass of notes and liberal coating of grime. You have been told to choose problems wherever you can find musty stacks of records based on trivial schedules prepared by tired bureaucrats. This is called "getting your hands dirty in real research." Those who counsel you are wise and honorable;

the reasons they offer are of great value. But one more thing is needful: first hand observation. Go and sit in the lounges of the luxury hotels and on the doorsteps of flophouses; sit on the Gold Coast settees and the slum shakedowns; sit in the Orchestra Hall and in the Star and Garter burlesque. In short, gentlemen, go get the seat of your pants dirty in real research.

The above passage offers an understanding of Park's efforts to entice his students to take up research through primary modes of investigation. For Park, both required researchers to immerse themselves with their research subjects as intensely as possible so that the facets of urban community life can be better understood in Chicago, which at that time experienced effects of massive growth of diverse peoples, new communities, changes in tradition and a cocktail of chaos and order of a burgeoning modern city. The directive set by Park has served as a crucial mainframe for global pioneering criminological ethnographies in urban locales (Whyte, 1943; Hobbs, 1988; Werdmölder, 1997; Anderson, 1999; Bourgois, 2003; Densley, 2013; Atkinson-Sheppard, 2019; Marsh, 2019). Here, it is important to note that the ethical standards in research have significantly evolved since The Chicago School. In the Western world, extensive emphasis is given on human interaction and safeguarding when pursuing research activities. Therefore, it would be naïve for researchers to apply Park's instruction without substantial ethical consequences. Moreover, beyond ethical barriers, in the last few decades, innovation-related research practice has become a focus for institutions. As such, the demand to produce research that is efficient and effective is preferred over traditional methods that can be viewed as outdated and archaic. Indeed, it is often technology that facilitates innovative research. We have discussed previously the role that technologies have played in some of our research experiences. Traditionally, qualitative researchers require less use of technology in comparison to their quantitative counterparts. However, in recent years, the emergence of artificial intelligence (AI) has drastically changed the convention of knowledge. Regardless of philosophical stance, AI has reoriented the discussion of ethics in research.

AI has widely been defined as a machine that can perform the cognitive functions that we typically associate with humans (Coeckelbergh, 2020; Liao, 2020; Boddington, 2023). Generally, in research, AI can be used for learning and problem solving. Academic research on the use of AI in scientific research largely explores the nature and extent of its use within scientific research. For example, Khlaif et al.'s (2023) study investigated the use of ChatGPT for scholarly work. They used ChatGPT to generate several articles and 50 abstracts, which were then thematically analysed for their scientific credibility and publishing quality. Their findings revealed that while ChatGPT has the potential to generate high-quality journals through detailed prompts, it only has a minor impact on literature reviews and data analysis. They also found concerns about the ownership and integrity of research with AI-generated text. Salvagno et al. (2023) also examined the use of ChatGPT for scientific writing within medical research. They noted that the use of ChatGPT should not substitute human judgement and found that the chatbot appears to be useful for assisting researchers in organising material and proofreading work. Their findings resonate with the author policy of Elsevier (n.d), a world leading journal that states on their website the below:

> *authors* are allowed to use generative AI and AI-assisted technologies in the writing process before submission, but only to improve the language and readability of their paper and with the appropriate disclosure, as per our instructions in Elsevier's Guide for Authors.

We do not intend to delve into an academic debate on the pros and cons of using AI platforms for research, considering the evolving nature of AI and the associated misinformation that currently occupies it. Rather, we are more concerned about the ethical implications of its use and its governance. We believe that there are several key ethical considerations that researchers should be aware of before engaging with AI for research-related matters.

1. **Plagiarism:** The acquisition of knowledge often encompasses the fusion of what one has learnt from others and their own critical input. In research, if the written work of others is repeated or reproduced through paraphrasing, there is a chance of committing plagiarism if the original authors are not appropriately referenced. As things currently stand, AI systems like ChatGPT can commit plagiarism under the definition offered in this chapter, even if they are programmed to avoid copying others by rephrasing their work in a manner that is similar to that of humans.

2. **The lack of criticality:** The absence of critical mass in research could result in hindering the growth of knowledge, which potentially has the impact of offering limited understandings of concepts, theories, and data. It can also exacerbate existing biases within the discipline. Given that AI-generated information is largely based on the initial user input, which is not critical to begin with, AI has a limited capacity to go beyond prevailing assumptions and understandings, ergo fails to evaluate information and associated prejudices. As such, we believe, a human expert in the field is crucial for ensuring quality in scientific activity and writing.

3. **Quantity over quality:** While AI tools can help writers write concisely and improve writing structure, we believe they pose a significant future risk of increasing publication numbers in some disciplines without increasing the experiences and expertise of scholars in those fields. Subsequently, publishing becomes a numbers game, whereby institutions

and disciplines may be at risk of hiring or assessing professionals based on the quantity of research outputs rather than quality.

4. **The black hole of data:** The use of AI software for research raises an array of GDPR (General Data Protection Regulation) issues. First, the collation and processing of data, particularly data concerning humans, must adhere to robust protocols pertaining to consent and data minimisation. Second, there is a risk that AI algorithms may unknowingly reveal sensitive information through the way they correlate data, thus potentially leading to breaches of privacy. Third, the use of AI makes it problematic for researchers to demonstrate transparency and accountability in decision-making, leading to damage in research integrity, professional reputation, and loss of trust from stakeholders.

Existing research on the governance of AI is largely beyond the remit of social sciences (see for example, Barocas & Selbst, 2016; Lipton & Steinhardt, 2018; Marda, 2018; Winfield & Marina, 2018). Cath's (2018) special issue paper explored governing AI and the associated ethical, legal, technical opportunities, and challenges. Some of the main concerns highlighted in the article pertain to the design and governance of AI in high-risk areas include: accountability, fairness, transparency, regulatory challenges, risk management, and legal compliance. Such concerns naturally fall within the remit of ethics. In addition, a concerning aspect of AI is its algorithmic approach to produce data (Selbst, 2017; Nemitz, 2018; Reisman et al., 2018). For instance, within criminal justice, automated databases are increasingly being used as decision-making tools to combat crime. However, serious concerns have been raised of their use and the biases that they generate, which have subsequently criminalised and stigmatised people from marginalised communities. A UK based example of this is the Gangs Matrix that was launched by the Metropolitan Police in 2012. It claimed to be a risk-management tool that focused on curbing serious violence, however, according to a report produced by Amnesty International (2018), the Gangs Matrix unfairly racially profiled young black men, of which consisted of a large population that had no previous criminal record. Amnesty International also raised concerns about data collection and how this interfered with young people's rights, as well as algorithmic data sharing between agencies connected with the Metropolitan Police.

Eubanks' (2018) compelling research on how government-driven high-tech tools profile and punish the poor in the US argues that automated decision-making has contributed to the widening of poverty in contrast to previous non-digital mechanisms, such as nineteenth-century poorhouses. Through several case examples, she persuasively concludes that automated decision-making has not only transformed how poor people are seen as lesser people, but sometimes barely as people at all. The two examples draw attention to the implications that algorithmic databases powered by AI have criminologically on society and its people. As such, we encourage that AI systems should be used with extreme caution by researchers. We stated in chapter one the 'consciousness' nature of AI, which has been largely theorised as artificial consciousness by scholars and widely defined as the ability of a machine to formulate autonomous intentions and make conscious decisions (Kok, 2009; Negrotti, 2012; Corea, 2017). Chalmers (2023) notes that a platform with similar operational capabilities such as ChatGPT may eventually have the capacity to review commonly accepted indicators of consciousness.

We therefore strongly believe that the use of AI will have major ramifications for academic research as its use by design will contribute to a moral input that will by default unsettle the foundation of conventional research ethics (i.e. decision-making, accountability, transparency, informed consent, security, data storage, etc). As such, we encourage that the governance of AI by all research ethics committees needs to be robustly assessed, as a recent review by Bouhouita-Guermech et al. (2023), which analysed 657 articles to review the challenges of AI in research ethics revealed that committees are struggling to respond to AI due to discrepancies between critical considerations across committee members, disproportionate focus on consent forms during review meetings, committee members lack of expertise on AI, and the lack of AI-specific standards and guidance to support research ethics practices worldwide.

Practical Recommendations

Below are several recommendations that we suggest will help the ethical mindfulness of researchers and wider stakeholders engaged in research activity.

Reflexivity as a Continuous Ethical Exercise

One of the main tools that we have discussed in the book that has helped us to produce rich ethically driven qualitative research is reflexivity. Given that reflexivity is 'a set of continuous, collaborative, and multifaceted practices through which researchers self-consciously critique, appraise, and evaluate how their subjectivity and context influence the research processes' (Olmos-Vega et al., 2022, p. 242), it enables researchers not only to only embrace their subjectivity but also to make nuanced and ethical judgements amid undertaking complex work to generate data that reflect the various dimensions of participants and social performances (Finlay, 2002). By taking inspiration from Olmos-Vega et al. (2022), who persuasively argue that reflexivity practically should address the researcher's personal, interpersonal, methodological, and contextual aspects throughout the research process, as well as combining our own experiences, we present below a multidimensional process that captures

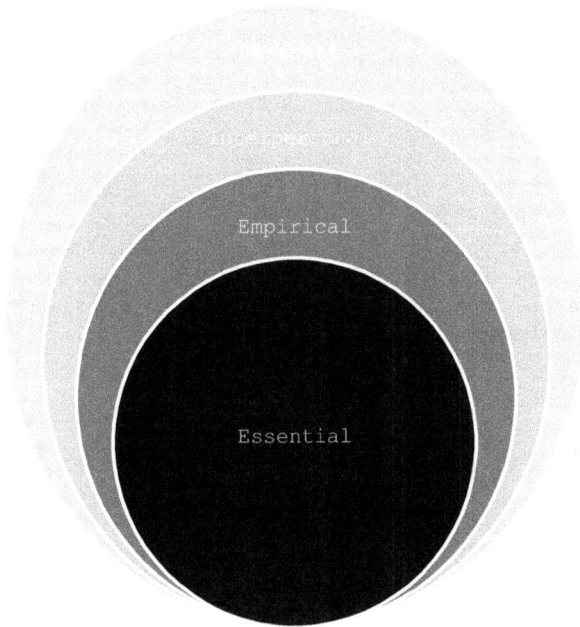

Figure 5.1 Reflexivity as a continuous ethical exercise: A multidimensional process

a holistic approach that will help researchers capitalise on reflexive practice throughout the duration of a research project.

The diagram above reinforces our standpoint that reflexivity goes beyond a mere self-reflection exercise of events; rather, it should be an ongoing concrete practice that is multidimensional. Our four interrelated dimensions of reflexive practice – essential, empirical, interpersonal, and personal – will not only assist researchers to produce high-quality, rigorous, and ethically sound research, but it can also be embedded within a broader understanding of reflexivity. We now outline and illustrate how these dimensions can be put into practice.

Essential reflexivity largely concerns itself with the governance of research ethics (see Chapter 2 for a more comprehensive breakdown). Here, it is important to note, to satisfy an ethics committee, researchers need to persuasively offer an understanding of:

• Research aims, objectives, and design.
• Participant selection and inclusion criteria.

- Risk assessment and mitigation of risk.
- Informed consent.
- Privacy and confidentiality.
- Community and cultural sensitivity.
- Research benefits.
- Research monitoring and review.

However, to effectively achieve the above, before filing for ethical approval, researchers need to first reflect on their own values, biases, and assumptions that may influence the objectives, design, criteria, and methods. They also need to consider the power dynamics that may occur when working with vulnerable cohorts. In addition, they need to undergo a reflexive assessment of potential risks and benefits, minimising the former and maximising the latter.

To achieve this, we encourage researchers to deliberate on the following questions that are quite epistemological in nature:

1. What knowledge do I possess for this topic and how did I acquire this knowledge?
2. How have my experiences and background shaped my thinking about the topic to date?
3. How do I currently perceive the cohort that I intend to study?
4. With what voice do I share my perspective?
5. Is it appropriate for me to undertake this study?

Empirical reflexivity challenges researchers to critically consider the intricacies and consequences of their methodological decisions, as well as having a mindfulness of disciplinary changes. We have both offered detailed insights on how we methodologically adapted our research projects in response to unforeseen circumstances (see, chapter two), or due to changes in participant interaction (see, chapter three). To produce successful qualitative research, researchers need to be attuned to the context, environments, and cultures that they intend to investigate. Important here is to note that qualitative research is often fluid and volatile, and any methodological decisions should not be finalised at the beginning of a project. Rather, reflexive researchers should train themselves to constantly assess, monitor and if need be, adapt their work to uphold ethics and rigour. Empirical reflexivity also lends itself to researchers having the capacity to consistently evaluate how their research contributes to the development of the discipline and broader societal impacts. This can include researchers undertaking regular tasks such as: keeping up to date with literature, being mindful of changes in legislation, policy, and funding, and being attuned to how their research can generate new knowledge that improves societal development. Being reflexive through a disciplinary lens can also help researchers appreciate the social, cultural, and historical context of the study. The questions below can help researchers embrace this mode of reflexivity:

1. Are my methods still feasible, and do they affect the ethical dimensions of my project?
2. Could my methods compromise the integrity of myself, my research team, and/or the integrity of my participants?
3. How does my research align or diverge with shared beliefs in the discipline?
4. What are the wider implications of my research?
5. What social, cultural, and historical dimensions affects my study?

Interpersonal reflexivity is arguably the most practised form of reflexivity by researchers. It generally relates to the relationship between the researcher, participants, and stakeholders. We have offered examples of this type of reflexivity when dealing with stakeholders (see Chapter 2), managing boundaries with participants (see Chapter 3), and the dealing of emotions when undertaking sensitive research (see Chapter 4). This mode of reflexivity is inherent in the research process, requiring researchers to be cognisant of how participants interpret questions, how the questions impact them, and how their insights shape decision-making and outcomes of the study. As discussed in Chapter 3, power imbalances are often inevitable between researchers and those researched. Interpersonal reflexivity helps in the review and analysis of power dynamics that take place between researchers, participants, and stakeholders. Given the convention of how research is conducted, it is often researchers that have authority on how data is interpreted and what information is viewed as valid. This enables them to hold a position of power and control relative to participants. Acknowledging and addressing all forms of power dynamics is pivotal for upholding ethical precepts and ensuring that data collection, its analysis, and its publication are conducted in a fair and transparent manner. The following questions are useful to contemplate when practising interpersonal reflexivity:

1. What impact is the research having on my participants?
2. What impact is the research having on me and the involved stakeholders?
3. What is informing the decision-making of my study?
4. What are the power imbalances in my research and how can they be mitigated?
5. How transparent are my encounters with participants?

Personal reflexivity, if practised correctly, this should be a continuous action that appears in all aspects of the research, from conception to output. Researchers are required to consider the impact of the research on themselves personally and professionally, and to discover how their reflections can foster learning and future change. By engaging in personal reflexivity, researchers can attain profound insights into their accountability, values, biases, assumptions, influences, growth, and development, ultimately enhancing the quality and rigour of their scholarly activities. The questions below serve as a good starting point for personal reflexivity:

1. How do these experiences align with my own values and ethics?
2. What influences have shaped my thoughts?
3. What has led me to this perception?
4. How have I and how do I continue to hold myself accountable?
5. What has been my contribution from beginning to end, and what is next for me?

Positionality Informed Research

We believe research to be a process not a product. This means to achieve concrete and ethically rigorous research; researchers need to engage in a series of actions and steps. One of the ways to acquire this is through an established research positionality. Research positionality is widely viewed as the subjective position and beliefs of the researcher within the research process. It considers the researcher's social, cultural, political, personal experiences, beliefs, biases, and affiliations that may influence how they conduct research (Bryman, 2016). We encourage researchers to consider the positionality of their research prior to its conception. This requires critically reflecting on oneself about the people and communities involved in the research and potential issues regarding power, privilege, and identity (Fenge et al., 2019). Naturally, positionality serves as a reflexive self-awareness exercise that enhances research credibility, impacts data collection and analysis, all while helping to address ethical concerns.

Recognising and establishing one's positionality during the start of a research project can subsequently inform and alter fieldwork. For example, if a qualitative study on the criminalisation of young people is conducted by a researcher who overlooks their positionality, the epistemic nature of their study will largely be guided by generic interpretivist principles. Conversely, a qualitative researcher approaching the same study from a critical race perspective would not only adhere to interpretivist principles but would also prioritise uncovering counter narratives (Breen, 2018). These narratives, valued by critical race scholars when studying marginalised communities, would represent individuals' experiences and perspectives, providing a rich resource for understanding their realities (Glynn, 2014).

One of the ways to effectively establish research positionality is through insider–outsider reflexivity. This often requires researchers to critically acknowledge their dual position as both an insider and outsider in a research context (see Chapter 3). Being an insider denotes common attributes, knowledge, and experiences with participants, while being an outsider implies a lack of familiarity (Bryman, 2016). Generally, researchers navigate between both positions to establish credibility, rapport, access, as well as interpret events in research settings. To practice insider–outsider reflexivity, researchers ideally need to regularly ask themselves the following questions:

1. What are my viewpoints about the subject under investigation philosophically, theoretically, and personally?
2. How will my race, class, gender, age, sexuality, politics, and faith affect my interaction with stakeholders and the wider research process?
3. What privileges do I occupy and how do they align or diverge with research stakeholders?
4. How is my dual position affecting the trajectory of my research?
5. Do I occupy the position of both insider and outsider rather than insider or outsider?

Multi-faceted Research Approach

We advocate researchers to use a diverse approach when carrying out qualitative criminological research. Indeed, we acknowledge that undertaking research that requires engaging with various methods and strategies to gather and analyse data from different perspectives can pose challenges in terms of feasibility, resources, and time. However, when studying human behaviour within their culture and society, employing several qualitative methods allows the production of compelling knowledge of how and why people interact the way they do. Similarly to our own experiences as criminological researchers (see, Deuchar, 2009, 2018; Deuchar et al., 2019; Rahman, 2016, 2019; Rahman et al., 2020), a swathe of academic literature that concerns the lived experiences of marginalised cohorts have used a blend of qualitative methods to better understand affective dimensions (i.e. moods, feelings, attitudes, values and motivations) of their participants (see, Anderson, 1999; Bourgios, 2003; Densley, 2013; Densley et al., 2023; Fraser, 2015; Hallsworth, 2013; Hobbs, 2013; McLean, 2019; McLean et al., 2019; McLean & Densley, 2022; Densley et al., 2023). Most of these studies have primarily strengthened their ethnographies with established primary and secondary qualitative methods such as: unstructured interviews, semi-structured interviews, surveys/questionnaires, case study research, focus groups, document analysis, life histories, and content analysis. Before finalising what methods to employ in their study, researchers need to ask themselves several critical questions to ensure that their choices align with their research goals, what is being studied, and what is ethically appropriate for their participants.

1. What method(s) can be used to appropriately answer my research question(s)?
2. What is the nature of the phenomenon under study?
3. What are the theoretical frameworks for the research?
4. What will be required to ensure research validity and reliability?
5. What are my strengths and weaknesses when carrying out research?
6. What level of involvement is required for the study?
7. What are the ethical considerations?
8. What are the practicalities?
9. What will be required to collect and analyse data?
10. What support can be offered to me to successfully complete fieldwork?

Ethical Governance of AI

A significant portion of this chapter considered an array of issues that AI presents when used for research. While the use of AI for academic research is currently in its infancy, it has become enticing for researchers to use to aid elements of their work. Floridi (2018) states that the digital revolution has reorientated our beliefs, values, behaviours, priorities as well as what sort of innovation is socially acceptable. While we accept that some may view AI to be extremely effective in assessing a situation and recommending a course of action that is consistent with previous ethical practice, the decision to adopt a course of action and its subsequent behaviour is fundamentally human. As such, the governance of this should be viewed as a major concern, especially when upholding research integrity. Therefore, it is crucial for university research ethics committees as well as committees beyond the higher education sector to develop a critical awareness of AI and the potential of its use. Beyond critical awareness, we believe that effective governance of AI and digital technologies requires nuanced consideration of ethical issues, engaging affected parties, and sharing solutions for best practices.

One effective governance approach is to have committees that are cross-functional, comprising of not only members that are subject specialists, but those that can identify and mitigate the risks of powerful technology. For instance, a social sciences research committee could benefit from including legal and technological experts alongside discipline specialists like anthropologists, criminologists, psychologists, and sociologists. As digital technologies evolve, it may become challenging to address bias, thus making what is legally permissible an important consideration. Conversely, while technologists may not be a subject specialist, they can help with the mechanical understanding of AI, aspects of risk mitigation, and feasibility. Furthermore, in the interest of transparency and accountability, it is crucial for any ethics committee to engage stakeholders involved in the use or potential use of AI for research. This could include the committee inviting the applicant(s) of a project to a meeting to address any concerns in person, especially if the research is sensitive in nature.

Having conversations in person allows stakeholders to actively listen and shows empathy to work through any challenges at hand. It also reduces misinterpretation, which we have often experienced as recurring when dealing with ethics committees. Lastly, given that AI is evolving rapidly, it is vital for committees and their members to share solutions with each other as well as with wider stakeholders. The benefits of doing so will foster a proactive learning environment, fill knowledge gaps, enable better judgement, and improve efficiency.

Chapter Summaries

This book has considered some of the prevailing philosophical, ethical, methodological, and practical elements associated with qualitative criminological research.

Chapter 1 offered the intricate relationship between ethics, philosophy, and research governance, particularly in the context of criminological research. It emphasised the significance of reflexivity as a continuous ethical exercise that holds researchers accountable for their actions and decisions throughout the research process. It highlighted the ethical considerations and challenges faced by researchers, institutions, and organisations, emphasising the need for adherence to ethical standards to protect participants, maintain research integrity, and prevent harm. By exploring the intersection of philosophy, ethics, and research governance, the chapter underlines the critical role of ethical conduct in producing credible, trustworthy, and socially responsible research outcomes in the field of criminology.

Chapter 2 underscored the importance of ethics in research, highlighting key aspects such as obtaining institutional ethical approval, ensuring participant confidentiality and anonymity, generating supporting documents, and addressing potential risks and benefits for participants. Through illustrative examples, this chapter also offered insights on how methodological dimensions of a study may evolve over time and how changes can be managed in a transparent, accountable, and ethical manner.

Chapter 3 offered rich narratives on how to ethically maintain boundaries in criminological research. Through several qualitative concepts, the chapter emphasises the importance for researchers to journey through blurred boundaries between themselves and participants while adhering to ethical and moral principles. It also drew attention through real-life cases the need to build rapport, trust, and empathy with participants to gather rich data but also offered caution on the extent to which researchers should engage emotionally. Using the insider–outsider approach, it considers dilemmas that researchers may face and the impact this has on criticality. The chapter concludes by discussing strategies for managing boundaries during fieldwork.

Chapter 4 largely focused on the emotional labour associated with criminological research by extensively discussing the importance of acknowledging and managing emotions when undertaking fieldwork. Yet again, through fieldwork examples, insights were offered on the emotional labour that was involved when studying reformed gang members and incarcerated members. The chapter underlines the gravitas for researchers to engage in emotional labour to manage what they encounter, especially when carrying out research on sensitive topics. To achieve this, the value of reflexivity and personal engagement with emotions in the research process was explored, ultimately advocating the need for engaging in emotional work so as to be able to protect the researcher from potential negative effects, as well as attaining a deeper understanding of the subjects being studied.

Here, in this final chapter (Chapter 5), we began by discussing how to ethically publish research. We then broadly explored the ethical parameters of research in a world that is increasingly becoming digitalised and influenced by AI. We are in no doubt that AI will eventually become a challenging social agent for researchers and their work. It is for this reason that we have stressed the importance for ethics committees and associated stakeholders to govern AI in an accountable, transparent, and moral manner. Fortunately, there are some aspects of qualitative research that AI technology will only have a small amount of influence on. As noted above, we recommend researchers to devote themselves to reflexive practice. Our multidimensional process and the associated questions for researchers to consider will equip them to produce high-quality, rigorous, and ethically sound research. Above all, it will train them to think critically with nuance, which AI fails to do. In addition to cultivating critical thinking, establishing a research positionality as well as conducting research through a multifaceted approach will empower researchers to make informed decisions while enhancing validity and comprehensiveness of their work.

Closing Comments

In closing, this book has journeyed the complex landscape of contemporary qualitative criminological research, revealing the essential nexus between philosophy, ethics, and methodological rigour. Each chapter has reflectively underlined the ethical imperative inherent in every aspect of research conduct, from the initial conceptualisation to the dissemination of findings in an increasingly digitalised world influenced by AI. Through narratives, reflections, and provocations, we have articulated the ethical challenges and responsibilities incumbent upon researchers, institutions, and society at large. As we head forward, where AI looms as a challenging force in research, we advocate for an unwavering commitment to reflexive practice. We see it not merely as a duty but as an ongoing ethical journey that has the power to empower, enlighten, and enrich those who earnestly embrace it. By nurturing critical thinking, cultivating research positionality, and embracing multifaceted approaches, qualitative researchers can navigate ethical dilemmas with sound judgement and integrity. We must remind ourselves to not relinquish our ethical compass amidst the surge of technological developments, but rather, we should commit to producing research that not only upholds the highest standards of rigour and credibility but also resonates with profound humanity and social responsibility.

References

Amnesty International (2018) *Trapped in the matrix: Secrecy, stigma and bias in the met's gangs database.* Available at: <https://www.amnesty.org.uk/files/2018-05/Trapped%20in%20the%20Matrix%20Amnesty%20report.pdf?VersionId=lJSxllcKfkZgr4gHZsz0vW8JZ0W3V_PD>. Last accessed: 9 March 2024.

Anderson, E. (1999) *Code of the street: Race and class in an urban community.* Chicago: University of Chicago Press.

Anderson, N. (1923) *The hobo: The sociology of the homeless man.* Chicago: University of Chicago Press.

Atkinson-Sheppard, S. (2019) *The gangs of Bangladesh: Mastaans, street gangs and 'Illicit child labourers' in Dhaka.* London: Palgrave.

Barocas, S., & Selbst, A. D. (2016). Big data's disparate impact. *California Law Review,* 104(3), 671–732.

Bernard, H. R. (2000) *Social research methods: Qualitative and quantitative approaches.* London: Sage.

Boddington, P. (2023) *AI ethics: A textbook.* Singapore: Springer.

Bouhouita-Guermech, S., Gogognon, P., & Bélisle-Pipon, J. C. (2023) Specific challenges posed by artificial intelligence in research ethics. *Frontiers in Artificial Intelligence,* 6, 1–16.

Bourgois, P. (2003) *In search of respect: Selling crack in El Barrio.* Cambridge: Cambridge University Press.

Breen, D. (2018) *Muslim schools, communities & critical race theory: Faith schooling in an islamophobic Britain?* London: Palgrave.

Bryman, A. (2016) *Social research methods.* Oxford: Oxford University Press.

Cath, C. (2018) Governing artificial intelligence: Ethical, legal and technical opportunities and challenges. *Philosophical Transactions of the Royal Society,* 376(2133), 1–8.

Chalmers, D. (2023) Could a large language model Be conscious? *New Orleans,* 28 November 2022. Available at: <https://arxiv.org/ftp/arxiv/papers/2303/2303.07103.pdf>. Last accessed: 11 March 2024.

Coeckelbergh, M. (2020) *AI Ethics.* Cambridge, MA: MIT Press.

Corea, F. (2017) *Artificial intelligence and exponential technologies: Business models evolution and new investment opportunities.* Cham Switzerland: Springer Nature.

Densley, J. (2013) *How gangs work: An ethnography of youth violence.* Oxford: Palgrave Macmillan.

Densley, J., McLean, R., & Brick, C. (2023) *Contesting county lines: Case studies in drug crime and deviant entrepreneurship.* Bristol: Bristol University Press.

Deuchar, R. (2009) *Gangs, marginalised youth and social capital.* London: Trentham Books.

Deuchar, R. (2018) *Gangs & spirituality: Global perspectives.* Switzerland: Palgrave MacMillan.

Deuchar, R., Crichlow, V. J., & Fallik, S. W. (2019) Cops in crisis?: Ethnographic insights on a new era of politicization, activism, accountability and change in transatlantic policing. *Policing and Society*, 30(1), 47–64.

Elsevier (n.d.) Publishing ethics. Available at: <https://www.elsevier.com/en-gb/about/policies-and-standards/publishing-ethics>. Last accessed: 7 March 2024.

Eubanks, V. (2018) *Automating Inequality: How high-tech tools profile, police and punish the poor*. New York: St Martin's Press.

Fenge, L. A., Oakley, L., Taylor, B., & Beer, S. (2019) The impact of sensitive research on the researcher: Preparedness and positionality. *International Journal of Qualitative Methods*, 18, 1–8.

Finlay L. (2002) Negotiating the swamp: The opportunity and challenge of reflexivity in research practice. *Qualitative Research*, 2(2), 209–230.

Floridi, L. (2018) Soft ethics and the governance of the digital. *Philosophy & Technology*, 376(2133), 1–11.

Fraser, A. (2015) *Urban legends: Gang identity in the post-industrial city*. London: Oxford University Press.

Glynn, M. (2014) *Black men, invisibility and crime: Towards a critical race theory of desistance*. London: Routledge.

Hallsworth, S. (2013) *The gang and beyond: Interpreting violent street worlds*. Hampshire: Palgrave.

Hobbs, D. (1988) *Doing the business: Entrepreneurship, detectives and the working class in the East end of London*. Oxford: Clarendon Press.

Hobbs, D. (2013) *Lush life: Constructing organized crime in the UK*. Oxford: Oxford University Press.

Khlaif, Z. N., Mousa, A., Hattab, M. K., Itmazi, J., Hassan, A. A., Sanmugam, M., & Ayyoub, A. (2023) The potential and concerns of using AI in scientific research: ChatGPT performance evaluation, *JMIR Medical Education*, 1–16.

Kok, J. N. (2009) *Artificial intelligence: Encyclopaedia of life support systems*. Oxford: Eolss Publishers.

Liao, M. (2020) *Ethics of artificial intelligence*. New York: Oxford University Press.

Lipton, Z. C., & Steinhardt, J. (2018) Troubling trends in machine learning scholarship: Some ML papers suffer from flaws that could mislead the public and stymie future research. *Association for Computing Machinery*, 17(1), 45–77.

Marda, V. (2018) Artificial intelligence policy in India: A framework for engaging the limits of data-driven decision-making. *Philosophical Transactions of the Royal Society*, 376(2133), 1–19.

Marsh, B. (2019) *The logic of violence: An ethnography of dublin's Illegal drug trade*. London: Routledge.

McKinney, J. C. (1966) *Constructive typology and social theory*. New York: Meredith Publishing Company.

McLean, R. (2019) *Gangs, drugs and (dis)organised crime*. Bristol: Bristol University Press.

McLean, R., & Densley, J. (2022) *Robbery in the illegal drugs trade: Violence and vengeance*. Bristol: Bristol University Press.

McLean, R., Robinson, G., & Densley, J. (2019) *County lines: Criminal networks and evolving drug markets in Britain*. Springer.

Negrotti, M. (2012) *Understanding the artificial: On the future shape of artificial intelligence*. Berlin: Springer-Verlag.

Nemitz, P. (2018) Constitutional democracy and technology in the age of artificial intelligence. *Philosophical Transactions of the Royal Society*, 376(2133), 1–14.

Olmos-Vega, F. M., Stalmeijer, R. E., Varpio, L., & Kahlke, R. (2022) A practical guide to reflexivity in qualitative research: AMEE Guide No. 149. *Medical Teacher*, 45(3), 241–251.

Park, R. (1915) The city: Suggestions for the investigation of human behavior in the city environment. *American Journal of Sociology*, 20, 577–612.

Rahman, M. (2016) Understanding organised crime and fatal violence in Birmingham: A case study of the 2003 new year shootings. Papers from the British Criminology Conference, Vol 16.

Rahman, M. (2019) *Homicide and organised crime: Ethnographic narratives of serious violence in the criminal underworld.* London: Palgrave.

Rahman, M., McLean, R., Deuchar, R., & Densley, J. (2020) Who are the enforcers? The motives and methods of muscle for hire in West Scotland and the West Midlands. *Trends in Organized Crime*, 25(2), 108–129.

Reisman, D., Schultz, J., Crawford, K., & Whittaker, M. (2018) Algorithmic impact assessments: A practical framework for public agency accountability. Available at: <https://www.nist.gov/system/files/documents/2021/10/04/aiareport2018.pdf>. Last accessed: 10 March 2024.

Salvagno, M., Taccone, F. S., & Gerli, A. G. (2023) Can artificial intelligence help for scientific writing?. *Critical Care*, 27(75), 1–5.

Selbst, A. D. (2017) Disparate impact in big data policing. *Georgia Law Review*, 52(1), 109–196.

Thrasher, F. (1927) *The gang: A study of 1,313 gangs in Chicago.* Chicago: University of Chicago.

Werdmölder, H. (1997) *A generation adrift: An ethnography of a criminal moroccan gang in the Netherlands.* Alphen aan den Rijn: Kluwer Law International.

Whyte, W. F. (1943) *Street corner society.* Chicago: University of Chicago Press.

Winfield, A. F. T., & Marina, J. (2018) Ethical governance is essential to building trust in robotics and artificial intelligence systems. *Philosophical Transactions of the Royal Society*, 376(2133), 1–13.

Wirth, L. (1928) *The Ghetto.* Chicago: University of Chicago Press.

Zorbaugh, H. W. (1929) *The gold coast and the slum: A sociological study of Chicago's near North Side.* Chicago: The University of Chicago Press.

Index

For Product Safety Concerns and Information please contact our EU
representative GPSR@taylorandfrancis.com
Taylor & Francis Verlag GmbH, Kaufingerstraße 24, 80331 München, Germany